MW00949616

Profiles of
PERSEVERANCE

Sustained by Hope in the Rough-And-Tumble of Real Life

A Study of Joseph, David, Elijah, and Nehemiah

MELANIE NEWTON

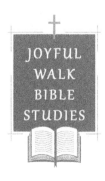

JOYFUL
WALK
BIBLE
STUDIES

We extend our heartfelt thanks to the many women who served as contributors to the original version of this study guide, especially Liz Church, Lori Schweers, Penny Semmelbeck, Brenda Baker, Lori Schweers, Robin Colley, and Jody Vise. Thanks also to Julia Gendron and the Thursday morning Bible Study group from Rockpointe Church whose weekly discussion of the lessons influenced this updated version.

For questions about the use of this study guide, please visit www.melanienewton.com to contact us.

Cover graphic is a public domain image of Mouro Island Lighthouse in Santander, Spain.

Published by Joyful Walk Ministries.

Scripture quotations unless otherwise noted are taken from the Holy Bible, New International Version ®, NIV ®. Copyright © 1973, 1978, 1984 by International Bible Society. Used by permission of Zondervan Publishing Company. All rights reserved.

Melanie Newton is the author of "Graceful Beginnings" books for anyone new to the Bible and "Joyful Walk Bible Studies" for established Christians. Her mission is to help women learn to study the Bible for themselves and to grow their Bible-teaching skills to lead others. For questions about the use of this study guide, please visit melanienewton.com to contact us.

We pray that you and your group will find *Profiles of Perseverance* a resource that God will use to strengthen you in your faith walk with Him.

JOYFUL WALK PRESS
Flower Mound, TX

MELANIE NEWTON

Melanie Newton is a Louisiana girl who made the choice to follow Jesus while attending LSU. She and her husband Ron married and moved to Texas for him to attend Dallas Theological Seminary. They stayed in Texas where Ron led a wilderness camping ministry for troubled youth for many years. Ron now helps corporations with their challenging employees and is the author of the top-rated business book, *No Jerks on the Job*.

Melanie jumped into raising three Texas-born children and serving in ministry to women at her church. Through the years, the Lord has given her opportunity to do Bible teaching and to write grace-based Bible studies for women that are now available from her website (melanienewton.com) and on Bible.org. *Graceful Beginnings* books are for anyone new to the Bible. *Joyful Walk Bible Studies* are for maturing Christians.

Melanie Newton loves to help women learn how to study the Bible for themselves. She also teaches online courses for women to grow their Bible-teaching skills to help others—all with the goal of getting to know Jesus more along the way. Her heart's desire is to encourage you to have a joyful relationship with Jesus Christ so you are willing to share that experience with others around you.

"Jesus took hold of me in 1972, and I've been on this great adventure ever since. My life is a gift of God, full of blessings in the midst of difficult challenges. The more I've learned and experienced God's absolutely amazing grace, the more I've discovered my faith walk to be a joyful one. I'm still seeking that joyful walk every day…"

Melanie

OTHER BIBLE STUDIES BY MELANIE NEWTON

Graceful Beginnings Series books for new-to-the-Bible Christians:

A Fresh Start: Beginning study for new Christians

Painting the Portrait of Jesus: A study of the Gospel of John

The God You Can Know: The character traits of our Father God

Grace Overflowing: Seeing Christ through a survey of Paul's letters

The Walk from Fear to Faith: Old Testament women

Satisfied by His Love: New Testament women

Seek the Treasure! Ephesians

Joyful Walk Bible Studies for growing Christians:

Graceful Living: The essentials of living a grace-based Christian life

Everyday Women, Ever Faithful God: Old Testament women (also in Spanish, Indonesian)

Live Out His Love: New Testament women

Heartbreak to Hope: Good news from Mark

Radical Acts: Adventure with the Spirit from the book of Acts

The God-Dependent Woman: Life choices from 2 Corinthians

Knowing Jesus, Knowing Joy: A study of Philippians (also in Spanish)

Healthy Living: A study of Colossians

Perspective: A study of 1 and 2 Thessalonians

Adorn Yourself with Godliness: A study of 1 Timothy and Titus (also in Spanish)

To Be Found Faithful: A study of 2 Timothy

Profiles of Perseverance: Old Testament men (also in Spanish)

Reboot, Renew, Rejoice: A study of 1 and 2 Chronicles

Connecting Faith to Life on Planet Earth: A study based on Genesis 1-11

Graceful Living Today: A 150-day devotional based on the Graceful Living study

Bible Study Leadership Courses

Bible Study Leadership Made Easy: Learn to lead with confidence & grace (online course)

The 5 C's of Small Group Leadership: Handbook for small group leaders

Find these and more resources for your spiritual growth at melanienewton.com.

Contents

Using This Study Guide

This study guide consists of 11 lessons covering the evidence of perseverance seen in the lives of four Old Testament men. For those who are not familiar with the history of Israel found in the Old Testament, each section begins with a brief history of a particular time period and then covers the life of 1 man who lived during that time.

The lessons are divided into 5 sections (about 20 minutes in length). The first 3 sections contain a detail study of the passages. The last section is a podcast that provides additional insight to the lesson. If you cannot do the entire lesson one week, please read the Bible passage(s) being covered.

THE BASIC STUDY

Each lesson includes core questions covering the passage narrative. These core questions will take you through the process of inductive Bible study—observation, interpretation, and application. The process is more easily understood in the context of answering these questions:

- What does the passage say? (**Observation**: what's actually there)

- What does it mean? (**Interpretation**: the author's intended meaning)

- How does this apply to me today? (**Application**: making it personal) *Your Life's Journey* questions lead you to introspection and application of a specific truth to your life.

STUDY ENHANCEMENTS

Deeper Discoveries: Embedded within the sections are *optional* questions for research of subjects we don't have time to cover adequately in the lessons or contain information that significantly enhance the basic study. If you are meeting with a small group, your leader may give you the opportunity to share your "discoveries."

Study Aids: To aid in proper interpretation and application of the study, five additional study aids are located where appropriate in the lesson:

- Historical Insights
- Scriptural Insights
- From the Hebrew/Greek (definitions of Hebrew/Greek words)
- Focus on the Meaning
- Think About It (thoughtful reflection)

Other useful study tools: Use online tools or apps (blueletterbible.org or "Blue Letter Bible app" is especially helpful) to find *cross references* (verses with similar content to what you are studying) and meanings of the *original Greek words or phrases* used (usually called "interlinear"). You can also look at any verse in *various Bible translations* to help with understanding what it is saying.

Because this study includes historical narratives set in various time periods, this is an excellent opportunity for you to learn how to use a Bible handbook, commentary, study Bible text notes or internet sources to discover information about the *time period* in which each person lived as well as the *towns, occupations, and other cultural information* that would add understanding to your study. We'll give you a few prompts at the beginning of the lessons.

PODCASTS

Find podcasts coordinating with these lessons at melanienewton.com/podcasts (choose "4: Profiles of Perseverance"). Or, follow the links in the PDF version to access the podcast for each lesson. Listen to the first podcast as an introduction to the study.

OLD TESTAMENT SUMMARY

About 1700 years after God created everything, He sent judgment on a rebellious race through a worldwide Flood. He later separated the nations with different languages and scattered them from Babel. Abraham, Isaac, and Jacob were founding fathers of the Hebrew people. Sold into slavery, Joseph became a powerful foreign leader.

The Israelites grew in number for ~400 years in Egypt. Then God delivered them from bondage through Moses who took the people across the Red Sea and taught them God's Law at Mt. Sinai. Joshua led the Israelites into the Promised Land after a 40-year trek in the wilderness because of unbelief.

During the transition toward monarchy, there were deliverer-rulers called "Judges," the last of whom was Samuel. The first three Hebrew kings—Saul, David, and Solomon—each ruled 40 years. Under Rehoboam, the Hebrew nation divided into northern and southern kingdoms, respectively called Israel and Judah. Prophets warned against worshipping the foreign god Baal.

After the reign of 19 wicked kings in the north, Assyria conquered and scattered the northern kingdom. In the south, 20 kings ruled for ~350 years, until Babylon took the people into captivity for 70 years. Zerubbabel, Ezra, and Nehemiah led the Jews back into Jerusalem over a 100-year period. More than 400 "silent years" spanned the gap between Malachi and Matthew.

The 39 books in the Old Testament are divided into 4 main categories:

- "The Law" (5 books)—the beginning of the nation of Israel as God's chosen people; God giving His Laws to the people that made them distinct from the rest of the nations.
- "HISTORY" (12 books)—narratives that reveal what happened from the time the people entered the Promised Land right after Moses died until 400 years before Christ was born.
- "POETRY & WISDOM" (5 books)—take place at the same time as the history books but are set apart because they are written as poems and have a lot of wise teaching in them.
- "PROPHETS" (17 books)—concurrent with the books of history and, except for Lamentations, reflect the name of the prophet through whom God spoke to the nation of Israel.

OLD TESTAMENT TIMELINE

Historical Period	Years BC.	Man Studied
The Patriarchs	2100 - 1800	Joseph
Israel in Egypt, Exodus, Conquest of Land	1800 - 1450	
Time of the Judges	1400 – 1000	
United Kingdom	1000 – 900	David
Divided Kingdom	900 – 586	Elijah
Restored Israel after Exile	538 – 400	Nehemiah

DISCUSSION GROUP GUIDELINES

1. **Attend consistently** whether your lesson is done or not. You'll learn from the other women, and they want to get to know you.

2. **Set aside time** to work through the study questions. The goal of Bible study is to **get to know** Jesus. He will change your life.

3. **Share your insights** from your personal study time. As you spend time in the Bible, Jesus will teach you truth through His Spirit inside you.

4. **Respect each other's insights**. Listen thoughtfully. Encourage each other as you interact. Refrain from dominating the discussion if you have a tendency to be talkative. ☺

5. **Celebrate our unity** in Christ. Avoid bringing up controversial subjects such as politics, divisive issues, and denominational differences.

6. **Maintain confidentiality.** Remember that anything shared during the group time is not to leave the **group** (unless permission is granted by the one sharing).

7. **Pray for one another** as sisters in Christ.

8. **Get to know the women** in your group. Please do not use your small group members for solicitation purposes for home businesses, though.

Enjoy your Joyful Walk Bible Study!

> **Recommended:** Listen to the podcast *"The Need for Perseverance"* at *melanienewton.com/podcasts* as an introduction to the whole study.

The Need for Perseverance

Jesus said to His followers that we will have trouble in this world (John 16:33). All of us. It doesn't matter where you live or how much money you have or what kind of success you have gained. It doesn't even matter how much faith you have or how faithful you have been to God in your daily life and work. Some troubles simply come from living in this fallen world and are common to everyone. Illness and natural disasters. Other troubles like persecution and rejection are related to being a child of God living in an unbelieving world. Then there are those we inflict upon ourselves because of sin still present within us—our own bad choices—or troubles that others inflict upon us because of their bad choices. Either way, we get stuck with the results.

So, in order to not only survive but also to thrive over a lifetime of ups and downs, you and I need to have something called **perseverance**, something the Bible says is good for us.

WHAT IS PERSEVERANCE?

- Perseverance is *holding to a course of action, a belief, or a purpose without giving way.* It refers to active staying power and tenacity to hold up under some long-term burden.

- The Greek word used often in the New Testament means "bearing under." It's holding up a load with staying power and tenacity. You have to be "under" to bear "under."

SUFFERING TESTS OUR FAITH; PERSEVERANCE MATURES OUR FAITH.

- The testing of our faith is on faith that is actually there. You can rejoice that you have faith worth testing (James 1:3).

- Jesus uses those tough times, when we are under stress, pain or suffering to reveal the parts of our character that are not so beautiful, not so strong, not so godly. And, if we let Him, He will remove that ugly stuff and strengthen what's left so we can **persevere.**

- When we persevere through any pain, distress, or long-term challenge, we will be mature, complete and lacking nothing (James 1:4). And, even have joy in the process because of the reward at the end for that staying power.

THE NEED FOR HOPE IN THIS DIFFICULT WORLD

- Hebrews 6:19 describes hope as an "anchor for the soul." It gives us security and stability like an anchor does for a ship in the midst of a storm.

- Biblical hope is not wishful thinking but *a confident, eager expectation of a coming certainty* based on the character of God to back up His promises. Our hope is rooted in the faithfulness of God. That hope enables us to persevere through the rough-and-tumble of real life.

- We live in the time period between Genesis 3 when sin entered the world and Revelation 21 when God does away with all sin and its effects. If we are going to **faithfully persevere**, we are going to have to accept this—not like it, but recognize it and not be discouraged.

THE CHOICE TO PERSEVERE

- You have to choose perseverance for it to finish its work. The opposite choice would result in whining, complaining, anger at God, and giving up.

- If we will let Him, Jesus will remove that yucky stuff to make us mature and complete, not lacking in anything **needed** necessary to live out Jesus' life in us.

- For you and me, God has things for us to do, kingdom work to do here on earth, during this time between Genesis 3 and Revelation 21. And, He needs us to be mature.

PREPARE BY INSTRUCTION, LEARN BY EXPERIENCE

- God's way of developing perseverance in our lives is this: "Prepare by instruction; learn by experience." Our instruction comes from the Bible, especially viewing the work of God in the lives of men and women during much of their lifetime. We can see God's faithfulness to them and be confident in His faithfulness to us as well. He is the same God.

  "For whatever was written in earlier times was written for our instruction, that through perseverance and the encouragement of the Scriptures we might have hope (Romans 15:4, NASB)."

- When we look at life just with our own eyes, we become fearful and pessimistic. We think to ourselves, "Nothing's going to work. I don't know if I can get through this." But, when we look at the Bible and see how God empowered everyday people like you and I to face their challenges, the Holy Spirit uses that scripture to strengthen us and to give us courage that we didn't know we had.

- God is the best teacher. So, we are going to look at the lives of several Old Testament believers to gain a long-term perspective about God's faithfulness to them as they persevered over many years, not just during a scene from their lives. We will discover what it means to be sustained by hope in the faithfulness of God, enabling us to persevere in the rough-and-tumble of life.

Do you want perseverance in your life? Consider these to be the lane markers for the race.

- #1. Choose to persevere through every challenge.
- #2. Count on God's promise to give you hope.
- #3. Let that hope sustain you through the rough-and-tumble of life.
- #4. Celebrate the joyful reward.

Let Jesus satisfy your heart with hope so you can persevere through life.

1 What Is Perseverance?

Hebrews 12:1–3; Romans 15:4

DAY ONE STUDY

The ABCs of Our Study—Author, Background, and Context

Like any book you read, it always helps to know a bit about the author, the background setting for the stories (i.e., past, present, future), and where the book fits into a series (that's the context). The same is true of Bible books.

AUTHORS

Unlike most of the New Testament books, we often do not know the authors of the Old Testament books, especially the ones of history. We will look at what we do know in the Historical Insights found at the beginning of lessons.

BACKGROUND AND CONTEXT

The books of the Old Testament (except for Genesis and Job) are the accounts of people living under the Old Covenant, the Law of Moses. It is important to keep that background and context in mind when studying them.

For example:

- "Salvation" (especially in the Psalms) usually refers to a temporal *deliverance* from trouble or danger, not regarding eternal life.

- A "judge" was like a hero or knight in shining armor, one who defended justice and the cause of the poor and defenseless, and often a military leader.

- "The Holy Spirit" came upon certain individuals *temporarily* to empower them for special service (such as artisans, prophets or kings) then left when that service was completed.

- "Forgiveness of sins" under the Law was accomplished through *atonement*, which means a "covering" for sin. A gracious God offered forgiveness to those who trusted in His lovingkindness, but it was at best *temporary* and *up-to-date*. Nowhere in the Law of Moses is there offered forgiveness for tomorrow's sins.

Throughout the Old Testament, God's grace accepted any person who came to Him by faith in Him. They received eternal salvation by their faith alone. That is consistent with what the New Testament teaches.

God's method of *managing* His people, however, was different, so *how* one's faith was expressed and lived out differed as well. The Tabernacle and the Temple represented the presence of God dwelling among His chosen people, Israel. There the priests represented the people to God, and sacrificial offerings were the prime way to publicly express worship, repentance, and thanksgiving. God wanted the worshiper's *heart* first. Where one's *heart* was right, sacrifices could be acceptable to God as an expression of inner faith. While we no longer express worship to God through animal sacrifices, He still desires the hearts of His people above all else.

When Jesus Christ died on the cross, He brought to a close the age of the Old Covenant, the Law of Moses, and simultaneously inaugurated the New Covenant in which we live. So, as you read the Old Testament books, read first to obtain accurate understanding of what their authors meant. Then, use New Testament teachings to apply truth about God to your everyday life in Jesus Christ.

1. What grabbed your attention as you read the background and context of any Old Testament study?

Sustained by Hope in the Rough-And-Tumble of Life

What is perseverance? By definition, "perseverance" is *holding to a course of action, belief, or purpose without giving way.* Perseverance, often used interchangeably with the word *endurance,* is the quality that enables a person to stand on his or her feet when facing a storm head on. It refers to active staying power and tenacity to hold up under some long-term burden, not just getting stuck in traffic. It carries the connotation of whole life experience.

By viewing the profiles (biographies) of Joseph, David, Elijah, and Nehemiah during much of their lifetime, we see God's faithfulness to them over many years, not just during a scene from their lives. By looking at their stories, we gain a long-term perspective through the rough-and-tumble of life. We can be encouraged to endure faithfully throughout our own rough-and-tumble life in this troubling yet exciting world. The Christian life is not a subject to be learned. Rather, it is a life to be lived.

Jesus said that we will surely have trouble in this world (John 16:33)—yes, even those of us who are faithful to Him. Whatever the struggles we face, we need a secure hope in order to "hang in there" over a lifetime of growing in His grace. The Christian life is not only **empowered by faith**; it is also **sustained by hope**. Only a secure hope rooted in the faithfulness of God enables us to weather the storms of life and persevere over a lifetime.

The writer of Hebrews pointed to the one focus in life that can give us hope that lasts, "keeping our eyes fixed on Jesus" (Hebrews 12:2). We must focus on what He is doing in the midst of what we are doing. It is our total confidence that Christ will complete the work He began in us that enables us to persevere through the rough-and-tumble of life.

By trusting a faithful God through present difficulties and pains, we can remain steadfast because we know the outcome. Christ will complete the work He began in us that enables us to persevere over a lifetime. We can persevere through the rough-and-tumble of life as we are empowered by our faith and sustained by our hope in an always faithful God.

Together, let's discover what it means to be sustained by hope in this rough-and-tumble life. Are you ready to develop perseverance in your life?!

> **Think About It:** You can't grow in grace in a classroom, through a seminar, or during a "quiet time," as good as those things may be...You can only grow in grace through a personal relationship with the Lord Jesus Christ, who teaches you truth from His Word, which you then take out into the rough-and-tumble of real life in the real world The "curriculum" cannot be planned or anticipated...Whatever the situations in *your* life may be, **that** is where you will have to grow in grace...in spite of our personal failures and sins... as we focus on what God is doing in the midst of what we are doing. (Bob George, *Growing in Grace,* pp. 13-15*)*

2. In the space below, write the definition of *perseverance* from the first paragraph of the explanation you just read. Remember this definition as you do this study.

Ask the Lord Jesus to teach you through His Word.

3. Write Hebrews 12:1-3 in the space below. These are our key verses for the whole study. We suggest that you work on memorizing these verses as you do your lessons.

What grabs your attention from these verses?

4. ***Your life's journey:*** What are you hoping to learn from this study? Where in your life do you need to develop perseverance?

Respond to the Lord about what He's shown you today.

DAY TWO STUDY

Read Hebrews 11:1-12:3. Ask the Lord Jesus to teach you through His Word.

Notice that the imagery used in 12:1 suggests an athletic contest in a great amphitheater with a dense cloud of witnesses. These are not spectators but those who can offer testimony of the value of putting faith in God even when you can't see the end. They lived that way. Just who are these witnesses?

5. Choose 5 of the "witnesses" in this chapter to list below by name or description. Pay particular notice to any challenging life circumstances given about them.

6. The job of a witness is to testify. According to Hebrews 12:1-3, their lives testified that perseverance is possible. The question then is "How?" To help you derive an answer, first reread Heb. 11:1, 6 then look for one phrase that is consistently used throughout the Hebrews 11 chapter. _____ How many times? _____

7. What does this tell you about how the witnesses persevered through all those challenging (or ordinary) life circumstances?

> **From the Greek:** The Greek word translated "endurance" or "perseverance" literally means "an abiding under; to abide." In other New Testament verses, it is translated "patience." Patience may be passive, that is, **endurance** under the general trials of life, Christian service or discipline. Patience may also be active (**perseverance**) involving persistence in well-doing, fruit-bearing and running the appointed race despite trials and distractions of life. (*Vines Complete Expository Dictionary*, pages 462-463)

Although the words *endurance* and *perseverance* may be used interchangeably, *perseverance* carries the connotation of whole life experience and is active. It is staying power. It is moving forward with the wind in your face trying to push you back or knock you over. It gives us a long-term perspective.

8. Back to Hebrews 12:1-3, who is to be our focus as we run this race with perseverance?

9. Read the following verses to answer this question, "What does it mean to fix your eyes on Jesus, and why should you?"

    • John 15:5—

    • John 14:6—

    • John 8:31-32—

10. Read the following quote. In the space below, explain why this analogy is a good one regarding a life of faith.

    Think About It: We are called first and foremost to a **Person**... There is a striking parallel between the baby's dependent relationship with its mother and our life of dependency on Christ. Because of its dependent life, a baby in the womb could say, "For me, to live is Mom." In the same way, we can say, "For me, to live is Christ." (Bob George, *Growing in Grace*, p. 78)

11. *Your life's journey:* Hebrews 12:1-2 refers to distractions that interfere with our running our "race of life" successfully. Think about things in your own life that are encumbrances or entanglements to you. What are they? No doubt they will be very similar to those distracting the people we will be studying through these lessons. Describe them through words or drawings in the space below.

Respond to the Lord about what He's shown you today.

DAY THREE STUDY

Ask the Lord Jesus to teach you through His Word.

12. The Christian life is pictured as a long-distance race rather than a short sprint. Read 1 Corinthians 9:24-27. How are we to run? Explain in your own words.

13. Read Philippians 2:14-16. What else do you learn about how we are to run our race?

14. Perseverance involves a choice. According to the following verses, what are the benefits of choosing to persevere all the way to the finish?

- Romans 5:1-5—

- 2 Timothy 4:6-8—

- James 1:2-4, 12—

Focus on the Meaning: Biblical hope is not wishful thinking but *a confident, eager expectation of a coming certainty* based on the character of God to back up His promises.

15. Read the following verses to answer this question, "What does God promise to us as we run the race?"

- Isaiah 43:1-3—

- Philippians 1:6—

- Romans 8:28, 38-39—

16. Read Romans 15:4. This is one of our key verses for this study along with Hebrews 12:1-3. How can we benefit from studying the lives of Old Testament people?

Our study will look at some of those witnesses mentioned in Hebrews 11, in particular, 4 Old Testament heroes whose lives were full of ups and downs. We will look at the circumstances challenging them year after year, what they believed about God and how that faith sustained them. **PERSEVERANCE** We will also see choices they had to make to remain faithful to God or not, and how each was affected by the choices. **PERSEVERANCE** Through their lives, we will glean truths about running with **PERSEVERANCE** throughout our entire lives as believers.

To develop perseverance in your life, let these be your lane markers for the race.

#1. Choose to persevere through every challenge.

#2. Count on God's promise to give you hope.

#3. Let that hope sustain you through the rough-and-tumble of life.

#4. Celebrate the joyful reward.

17. ***Your life's journey:*** How might choosing to persevere in your life give you real hope *(a confident, eager expectation of a coming certainty)* for today and for the future?

> **Think About It:** Living by faith is a life of total dependency, objectivity (Christ is trustworthy as the object of our faith) and availability. We live in total dependency upon the Person of the crucified and risen Christ, and we step out by faith in the objective truth of His written Word, trusting Him for the ability to do what He wills, and entrusting Him with the results of our actions. (Bob George, *Growing in Grace*, p. 86)

Respond to the Lord about what He's shown you today.

Recommended: *Listen to the podcast "Stay Focused on Jesus" after doing this lesson to reinforce what you have learned. Use the listener guide on the next page.*

Stay Focused on Jesus

Hebrews 12:1-3 uses the imagery of running a long race like a marathon. The setting is that of an athletic contest in a great amphitheater with a dense cloud of witnesses—not spectators—but those who can testify to the value of putting your faith in God even when you can't see the end. They lived that way. They ran that race.

The race is the rough-and-tumble of real life. Real life hurts. It's confusing. It blindsides us. We often cling to things that hinder us. We have to make the choice to throw off everything that entangles us and keeps us from running the race with perseverance.

THROW OFF WHAT HINDERS US

- Perseverance is active staying power and tenacity to hold up under some long-term burden. Expect a difficulty to be long-term and a burden.

- If you expect that a Christian life should have fewer trials except those brought on by yourself, that is unrealistic and dangerous thinking because it leads to continual disappointment. That is a hindrance.

- Other hindrances are our own bad choices that bring trouble to us. Or, the bad choices of others that are inflicted upon us. Either way, we get stuck with the results. Those can be hindrances.

PERSEVERANCE PRODUCES MATURITY IN US

- God's goal for us is to be mature and complete. Perseverance is His tool to help us reach that goal.

- We don't naturally desire perseverance. We get sidetracked with our comforts and our rights. Without perseverance, we become satisfied with immaturity.

  "Consider it pure joy, my brothers and sisters, whenever you face trials of many kinds" (James 1:2)

- Most people count it all joy when they escape trials, and they count it all grief when they have to endure them. But, God's not going to overprotect His children.

- THE KEY: Human parents raise their children to be less dependent on them and more independent as they grow up. But, God raises His children to be *less independent of Him* and ***more dependent on Him.*** Whatever He brings into our lives that makes us more dependent upon Him is good for us. If He didn't bring those things into our lives, we wouldn't know how to rely on Him for real strength.

STAY FOCUSED ON JESUS

- Christianity is Christ! It's not a lifestyle, rules of conduct, or a society whose members were initiated by the sprinkling or covering of water. We are called first and foremost to a relationship with a **Person—Jesus Christ**.

- When we stay focused on Jesus, we know we are not alone. We have a Savior who has run this race of life already. He knows how hard it is. He knows how to persevere through it. We can trust Him.

- Be tenacious to hold onto Jesus. Go wherever Jesus leads you to go. Persevere. Focus on what He is doing in the midst of what we are doing. Listen to His voice, drowning out all the others. Even when it hurts. When you're tired. When you want to give up. When you want to settle for less. Believe it or not, persevering through the really tough times will lead to a joyful run through this race of life with Him.

We can have hope because we have God with us. So, remember our lane markers for the race.

#1. Choose to persevere through every challenge.
#2. Count on God's promise to give you hope.
#3. Let that hope sustain you through the rough-and-tumble of life.
#4. Celebrate the joyful reward.

Let Jesus satisfy your heart with hope so you can persevere through life.

Joseph—A Man of Faith

2 Responding to Rejection & Loss

Genesis 37 & 39

For whatever was written in earlier times was written for our instruction, that through perseverance and the encouragement of the Scriptures we might have hope (Romans 15:4, NASB)

DAY ONE STUDY

Historical Perspective: "The Patriarchs"

The term *patriarch* denotes the father or male leader of a family or tribe. When used in Biblical studies, it usually refers to the three main characters in Genesis chapters 12 through 50—Abraham, Isaac, and Jacob. Under God's direction, Abraham left Ur in Mesopotamia, with its culture and conveniences, for the land of Canaan. Patriarchal life was seminomadic meaning they wandered from place to place, searching for grazing land and water for their animals. They measured their wealth in livestock and movable goods such as silver, gold, and tents.

Through Abraham and his descendants, God began to develop a people of His own. The Abrahamic Covenant contains many precious promises: Abraham would have numerous offspring; his descendants would possess the land of Canaan; and the Messiah would come forth one day from his line. These promises passed on to Abraham's son Isaac and then to Isaac's son Jacob (whom God later renamed Israel). Jacob's sons formed the nucleus of the twelve tribes of Israel.

Joseph is the long-awaited son born to Jacob and his beloved wife Rachel. After many years of childlessness for Rachel, Joseph is born into an extended family of ten stepbrothers. Later, Rachel dies while giving birth to her second son—Joseph's younger brother Benjamin. Joseph is deeply loved by his father and closely bonded to Benjamin. Jacob's 12 sons were the ancestors of the nation of Israel, the people through whom God sent His Son, Jesus.

Moses is credited with being the author of the first five books of the Bible—Genesis, Exodus, Leviticus, Numbers and Deuteronomy. For Genesis, it is thought that he compiled the journals handed down by those who came before him. You'll see various times in Genesis the phrase, "This is the account of..." We see that in Genesis 37:2 regarding Jacob's family line.

> **Recommended:** *Read or listen to Genesis chapters 37-50 to get the "Big Picture" of Joseph's life during this study.*

Read Genesis chapter 37. Ask the Lord Jesus to teach you through His Word.

1. ***Deeper Discoveries (optional):*** Find out more information about the time period in which Joseph lived.

   - The many uses of a cloak—

   - Caravans—

- The Midianites—

- The job of a household manager—

2. Focus on Genesis 37:1-11. Describe the nature of Joseph's relationship with his father and older brothers.

3. How do Jacob and Joseph both contribute to the seething resentment of Joseph's brothers?

4. Focus on Genesis 37:11-36. Describe what happens to Joseph, including the motivation behind such cruel treatment.

Think About It: Although Joseph's brothers didn't kill him outright, they wouldn't expect him to survive for long as a slave. They were quite willing to let cruel slave traders do their dirty work for them. Joseph faced a 30-day journey through the desert, probably chained and on foot. He would be treated like baggage, and once in Egypt, would be sold as a piece of merchandise. His brothers thought they would never see him again. (*Life Application Study Bible,* note on Genesis 37:28)

5. What did God provide to rescue Joseph?

Think About It: Acts 7:9 says that God "rescued" Joseph. Would you consider being sold into slavery in a foreign country as a rescue?

6. We get a glimpse of Joseph's reaction to all of this in Genesis 42:21. What does he remember about this?

> **Think About It:** Joseph didn't know how the story would turn out. The most he knew were the dreams he had as a kid. Living by faith is a lot in the dark. All he could do is trust God, and in the process, he got to know God and see the fruit of trusting Him.

7. ***Your life's journey:*** In Genesis 39:2, we see these words, "The Lord was with Joseph." The Bible says that difficulties are a part of life, even for His children (Matthew 7:24). He also promises us that He will be with us in our darkest hour, just as He was with Joseph. Read the following verses. What is promised to help sustain you in dark times?

    *   Deuteronomy 31:6 —

    *   Psalm 118:5-9 —

    *   Isaiah 40:27-31 —

Respond to the Lord about what He's shown you today.

DAY TWO STUDY

Read Genesis 39:1-6. Ask the Lord Jesus to teach you through His Word.

Joseph is taken to Egypt, and purchased by Potiphar, who is captain of the guard for Pharaoh. In a short period of time, 17-year-old Joseph had been forcibly taken from his adoring father and a simple, rural environment to endure slavery in a foreign land and culture—all from the hands of his own brothers.

8. Focus on Genesis 37:36 and 39:1. What adjustments did Joseph need to make …

   • Physically?

   • Mentally?

   • Emotionally?

9. Considering typical human nature, what potential reactions toward God might Joseph have experienced during this distressing time?

Scriptural Insight: Where would Joseph have learned about God? He had no written Old Testament. Yet, we are told 10 times in Genesis that the various patriarchs kept written accounts of what happened during their lifetimes. You can see reference to these accounts in Genesis 2:4; 5:1 (specifically says "written"); 6:9; 10:1; 11:10, 27; 25:12, 19; and 36:1, 9. Moses took these accounts and compiled them into the book we know as Genesis. Joseph would have heard stories about his great grandfather Abraham's encounters with God and God's promises to Abraham's descendants. Joseph would have heard about God's faithfulness to his own father Jacob. Jacob had several personal interactions with God (see Genesis 35), including a dream (Genesis 28:10-22) and an all-night wrestling match (Genesis 32:22-32). Whatever Joseph had been taught about God, he learned that God was worthy of worship, that sin against God is bad, and that God could be trusted in all situations. Joseph's choice to follow God is no different than yours is today. Act on what you know!

Joseph was rejected, betrayed and abandoned by his own family. His status changed in an instant from favored son in Canaan to anonymous slave in the house of an Egyptian. Notice that there is no mention of *time* in verses 1-6. We have no idea how long Joseph labored for Potiphar as these events began to unfold. It could have been months or it could have been up to 8 *years*.

10. At this vulnerable point in his life, Joseph could have easily given in to despair and hopelessness.

   • Instead, what did he choose to do?

- What does this response to such harsh, bewildering circumstances in his life demonstrate about Joseph?

11. How does God respond to His faithful servant Joseph (vv. 2-6)?

12. What did God NOT do that Joseph might have longed for Him to do?

13. *Your life's journey:* Consider a time when you chose (exercised your will) to respond with faithfulness to God despite difficult circumstances in life.

- How was God faithful to you? In what ways did He encourage you?

- How can *you* encourage someone who is struggling with this right now?

Think About It: Fill your mind with the thought that God is there. And once your mind is truly filled with that thought, when you experience difficulties it will be as easy as breathing for you to remember, "My heavenly father knows all about this!" (Oswald Chambers, *My Utmost for His Highest,* July 16)

Respond to the Lord about what He's shown you today.

DAY THREE STUDY

Read Genesis 39:1-19. Ask the Lord Jesus to teach you through His Word.

Throughout his difficult ordeal, Joseph chose to trust God with everything that was happening to him. Therefore, he was able to carry on with his life, endeavoring to do his best in everything that was required of him. His efforts were blessed by God and noticed by Potiphar, who eventually entrusted *everything* to Joseph's care. Then, as Joseph is honored with power and authority, he is forcefully confronted with temptation. This occurs between 1 and 8 years of Joseph getting to Potiphar's house.

14. Look at Joseph's predicament in vv. 6-10. What conflicting emotions would Joseph have had while being pursued by Potiphar's insistent wife day after day?

Focus on the Meaning: Temptation is a fact in God's world. Temptation itself is not sin. It is something we are bound to face simply because we are human with a sinful nature in a fallen world controlled by someone who hates God (Satan).

15. How did Joseph deal with this seductive temptation?

16. From vv. 11-15, when trapped, what did he do?

Scriptural Insight: Joseph is a shining example of one who, by faith, trusted God and did what he should. And it cost him big! But, only for a season. One can never out do God. His reward is always more satisfying than how we might try to satisfy ourselves. First, Joseph tried to prevent the problem by not being alone in the house with Potiphar's wife. When she trapped him, he didn't take the bait. He immediately fled the situation; no negotiation, no flirtation, just evacuation! He didn't entertain the idea of immorality even for a moment. It is God's desire that His people be morally pure (1 Thessalonians 4:1-8). We are to flee sexual immorality. We are not to flee sex! Sex is a marvelous and joyous experience when kept within God's boundaries. Christians should hold to a higher view of sex than the world does.

17. What does Joseph's responses to the temptations demonstrate about his attitude …

- Toward sin?

- Toward God?

- Toward those who trust him?

18. Read Hebrews 2:17-18 and 4:15-16. Why can we trust our God to sustain us in the midst of life's temptations?

19. God also promises to give us a way to escape temptation. Read 1 Corinthians 10:13. Write this verse in the space below.

20. **Your life's journey:** Think of a common temptation for you. When you are tempted to do that, what practical steps do you take to not fall into sin?

Respond to the Lord about what He's shown you today.

Recommended: *Listen to the podcast "God Is with You in the Pit" after doing this lesson to reinforce what you have learned. Use the listener guide on the next page.*

God Is with You in the Pit

If you are in a time of life that is without crisis, now is the time to bulk up. Before a long race or big game, athletes are told to bulk up so that they will have energy to sustain them to the finish. Bulk up in the knowledge of God and in your relationship with God so that you will function well. That starts with knowing who God is and why you can trust Him with your crisis. He may not rescue you from every threatening situation, but there are 4 truths you can count on to get you through every single one of them.

1) God loves you.
2) God knows what is going on in your life.
3) God can do something about it.
4) You can trust His goodness in what He chooses to do.

THE PIT OF REJECTION

- Joseph had a knowledge of God, a trust in Him, and a desire to be obedient to Him before he ever got thrown into the pit.

- Joseph's brothers attack him, throw him into a pit, and sell him to slave traders. They turned a deaf ear to Joseph's distress and pleading for his life. But, God rescued Joseph by sending that caravan at just the right time, going to the right place, and with those willing to buy this teenager for future sale.

- Rejection by family hurts. Jesus gets your pain. He knows exactly how you feel. You can tell Him all about it as you fix your eyes on Him. Jesus will comfort your heart and help you heal.

THE PIT OF LOSS

- Joseph lost time with a loving father, his youth, his inheritance as the son of a wealthy landowner, and his freedom. Most of that could never be restored.

- The reality is that all the people in the Bible were real people with emotions and feelings just as we have today.

- We are quick to quote Romans 8:28, wanting that verse to mean that God will fix it so everything turns out rosy for our lives.

- Being in that pit hurts. We must live with the loss and move on. Joseph chose to function well in the pit of loss. He used his skills and abilities to persevere through it because he realized that God was with him in that pit.

GOD IS WITH YOU IN THE PIT

- God was with Joseph, actively involved for good in Joseph's life. In the pit. In the rejection and loss. In the servitude and prison. He had God. He didn't need anything or anyone else.

- Joseph didn't know how the story would turn out. All he could do is trust God, and in the process, he got to know God and see the fruit of trusting him. Joseph chose to function well. Perseverance is functioning well in the pit.

- Most of the time we can't see the reason why we went through an experience until a resolution comes. Then, we can step back and see how God helped, guided and comforted us through it all. But, for some situations, we may never know the reason until we get to heaven. No matter what happens to us on this earth, we know we will live a life of eternal joy and praise in God's presence in heaven. This fact can comfort us and give us hope while we wait for that day.

- So, how do you persevere in the pit of rejection and loss? Whether you feel it or not, know that God is with you! He loves you, He knows what is going on in your life, He can do something about it, and you can trust His goodness in whatever He chooses to do.

We can have hope because we have God with us. So, remember our lane markers for the race.

- #1. Choose to persevere through every challenge.
- #2. Count on God's promise to give you hope.
- #3. Let that hope sustain you through the rough-and-tumble of life.
- #4. Celebrate the joyful reward.

Let Jesus satisfy your heart with hope so you can persevere through life.

Joseph—A Man of Faith

3 Responding to Waiting

Genesis 39-41

For everything that was written in the past was written to teach us, so that through the endurance taught in the Scriptures and the encouragement they provide we might have hope. (Romans 15:4, NIV)

DAY ONE STUDY

Read Genesis 39:19-23. Ask the Lord Jesus to teach you through His Word.

1. ***Deeper Discoveries (optional):*** Find out more information about the time period in which Joseph lived.

   • Cupbearer—

   • Signet rings—

   • Egyptian storehouses—

Joseph remained faithful to God in the midst of temptation, but suffered unjustly for it and was sent to prison for a crime he didn't commit. This is the second time that Joseph's cloak was used to bring a false report about him. He ended up in bondage both times. Joseph was in a prison where the king's prisoners were kept. It was not the worst place but still called a dungeon in Genesis 41:14. Yet, it was the place where God rescued Joseph once again from a bad situation.

2. How did God encourage Joseph in the midst of such bitter, unfair circumstances?

Focus on the Meaning: Temptation is the oldest of all the inner conflicts in the human heart, and the battle against it is a hard fought one. Although temptation may lead to sin, being tempted is not sin. Everyone, including Jesus, has struggled with it, but Jesus is the only person who hasn't suffered the consequences of yielding to it (see Matthew 4:1-11). Regardless of how temptation is "packaged," it always entices us to step out of our faith relationship with God and believe that we can't trust Him with the timing and the result of our predicament. If our situation is difficult, we can fall into the trap of

27

concluding that God isn't good and loving or that He doesn't care about the hardships we are facing. Our tendency is to demand instant relief from our situation, choosing to give up on God rather than persevering, through faith, amidst the difficulties and/or drudgery of life.

3. *Your life's journey:* Have you, like Joseph, ever been faithful to God despite tremendous personal cost? How did God encourage you in your situation? Consider writing a poem of thankfulness for His faithfulness to you.

Respond to the Lord about what He's shown you today.

Day Two Study

Read Genesis chapter 40. Ask the Lord Jesus to teach you through His Word.

4. Let's look at what happened to Joseph in prison.

 • What happened in vv. 1-5?

 • What did Joseph notice about them and say to them (vv. 6-8)?

 • After interpreting the dream, what does he say to the cupbearer (vv.14-15)?

 • What did the cupbearer do (v. 23)?

5. Two full years passed after this incident (Genesis 41:1). Based on what you've learned about Joseph, what was he doing during that two years of waiting?

6. What did Joseph learn during his long period of "darkness" that prepared him for the incredible "dawn" he would eventually experience? See also Acts 7:9-10.

Think About It: The dross of our character—pride, rebellion, and self-sufficiency—melts in the crucible called waiting. Yet it is a crucible that we do everything to avoid. We even have a cultural myth that says to wait is to waste time ... And even though suffering may force us to slow down, to wait, we complain and seek solace in mindless distractions and miss the refining of our character that God intended. (Chuck Swindoll)

7. *Your life's journey:* Think about those times when you consider waiting a waste of time.

- Read 1 Peter 5:10. What does God promise?

- If you are currently in the "crucible of waiting," consider the verse you just read and ask God to help you see **His work in your character** with the following question: "What in my character does God need to perfect or strengthen in me?"

Think About It: God is in the waiting, too, right along with you. He needed to wait until the right conditions were in place before He could move Jacob and clan to Egypt. That took ~22 years of waiting on His part. Jesus had to wait for more than 10 years after He became a man for the time to be ripe to begin His ministry. During that time, Jesus worked alongside His father in the family business, functioning well. Jesus understands how you feel when you are "in the waiting."

DAY THREE STUDY

Read Genesis chapter 41. Ask the Lord Jesus to teach you through His Word.

Falsely accused of attempted rape, Joseph remains in prison, forgotten by everyone (except God). He has now been a slave in Egypt for ~13 years. Despite the incredible wait, Joseph refuses to allow discouragement to imprison his heart and make him lose hope. Then, the time is right for God to put His plan for all of Israel into action. Pharaoh has two dreams. No one can interpret them. The cupbearer remembers Joseph.

8. Let's look at how God dramatically secures Joseph's release from prison in vv. 14-40.

   • After hearing Pharaoh's request, what is Joseph's response (v. 16)?

   • What did God show Pharaoh through the dreams (vv. 25-32)?

   • What wise counsel did Joseph give (vv. 33-36)?

   • What does Pharaoh see in Joseph (vv. 37-40)?

9. Focus on vv. 41-57. How does God exalt Joseph and bless Egypt? See also 1 Peter 5:6.

10. In vv. 16-57, how often does Joseph deliberately give glory to God? Give verses where Joseph verbally did this.

11. How did Joseph's work for Potiphar and the prison warden prepare Joseph for his most important job?

In today's society, Joseph "lost" 13 years of his life and would have been considered a "victim" of unjust circumstances—a man whose personal "rights" had been ignored or violated. But in reality, Joseph was a "victor." For *13 years* God tested and refined Joseph's faith. Then, when Joseph had proven himself faithful to God throughout everything that happened to him, God exalted him. When life gets you down, and you are tempted to "give up" on God and take matters into your own hands, remember:

- *Who God is.* He is God, and I am not. He is creator of the universe and all mankind; He knows me and loves me and sees my situation; nothing is hidden from Him.

- *Agree that God knows what He is doing.* He has a greater purpose for me in the midst of my difficult situation. Although I may not see it right now, like it, or understand it, I can trust his character. His word is true, and He will honor his promises and meet my needs.

- *Let your actions be based on the truth of God's Word*, not your feelings or emotions which can lead you astray. Depend on Jesus for the power to persevere, and trust Him with the results.

12. **Your life's journey:** How does the above information encourage you? How can you apply it to your life? Consider transferring the truths to a note card to keep handy for the next time you need to be reminded of them.

Respond to the Lord about what He's shown you today.

> **Recommended:** Listen to the podcast *"God Is with You in the Waiting"* after doing this lesson to reinforce what you have learned. Use the listener guide on the next page.

God Is with You in the Waiting

Joseph found himself in prison. At this point in his life Joseph was left with two choices: 1) go through the situation on his own or 2) by faith go through it with God. God always responds to people of faith. Believe it or not, prison was once again God's rescue of Joseph from a bad situation.

And, God was with him there. God showed him kindness there. And granted him favor in the eyes of the prison warden. Joseph chose to persevere there and function well there. In the prison. In the confinement. Not of his choosing. But, where he found himself to be. That's where he needed to trust God and function well. It was a place not only of rescue from the bad situation but also a place of maturation for Joseph's future. A place of waiting. And, God was in the waiting, too.

GOD IS IN THE WAITING

> "You are in the waiting in that moment of my life, when my faith and hope collide. My heart's anticipating just how and when You'll move. Oh, that's when You prove You are in the waiting too" ("In the Waiting" by Shannon Wexelberg)

- God waited 22 years until the right conditions were in place before He moved Jacob and clan to Egypt.

- Jesus waited for more than 10 years after He became a man for the timing to be ripe, to be perfect, to begin His ministry. During that waiting time, Jesus worked alongside His father in the family business. Like Joseph, He functioned well. Jesus understands how you feel when you are "in the waiting."

WAITING BINDS US TOGETHER WITH THE LORD

- The Hebrew word most commonly used to wait upon the Lord is a word that means "to hope and expect." It also means "to bind together as in tying together loose ends." How does waiting bind us together with the Lord?

- Waiting on the Lord will make us stronger because waiting teaches us about God and His timing. *"I will watch expectantly for the Lord (Micah 7:7)."* During those times of waiting, our ear is more attuned to how God is working. That binds us with Him.

- Waiting on the Lord makes us available to talk with Him in prayer. When we seek God for a solution in our lives, these times of waiting strengthen our relationship with Him as we learn to rely on His timing and trust in His goodness. It binds us together with Him.

- Waiting does not mean to just do nothing. While we are trusting Him, we continue moving forward, functioning well in life. Just like Joseph did.

- Waiting doesn't just bind us together with God but also prepares us for what is next.

WAITING PREPARES US FOR WHAT IS NEXT

- During the time of waiting, Joseph learned that it pays to have a good reputation. He became more efficient at managing people and supplies. He trusted God more and recognized God's presence with him. He learned how to function well in the midst of loneliness, opposition, temptation, restriction, disappointment, success, and opportunity.

- Joseph had to wait patiently for God to act. We also must wait for God's "always perfect" timing in answer to our prayers.

If you consider that God is in the waiting with you and that waiting binds you together with Him, does this change your perspective of waiting? It could be God rescuing you from a bad situation. Or, God preparing you for a specific task that will impact many people. It could be God teaching you how to trust Him and rely on Him more than on yourself. And, He is in that waiting, too. That should give you hope.

We can have hope because we have God with us. So, remember our lane markers for the race.

#1. Choose to persevere through every challenge.
#2. Count on God's promise to give you hope.
#3. Let that hope sustain you through the rough-and-tumble of life.
#4. Celebrate the joyful reward.

Let Jesus satisfy your heart with hope so you can persevere through life.

Joseph—A Man of Faith

4 God Meant It For Good

Genesis 42-46; 50:15-22

For everything that was written in former times was written for our instruction, so that through endurance and through encouragement of the Scriptures we may have hope. (Romans 15:4, NET)

DAY ONE STUDY

Pharaoh's terrible dream is realized. A severe famine grips the Earth. Joseph, as Pharaoh's prime minister, has wisely prepared his country for the oncoming devastation, and Egypt is a land of plenty. Back in Canaan, Joseph's family is starving. His brothers (except for Benjamin) journey to Egypt to buy grain. More than 20 years have passed since they threw Joseph into a pit. Joseph now lives as an Egyptian in dress and speech, and his desperate brothers do not recognize him as they stand before this powerful official, needing to get food. But Joseph recognizes them. One can only imagine his shock as he looks at them.

Read Genesis 42:1-28. Ask the Lord Jesus to teach you through His Word.

Much of the Bible is written in narrative form. That's what you find here in Genesis and the other books of history. Narrative is *descriptive* not prescriptive. What do I mean by that?

> *Descriptive* = observation of what actually happened, how people lived and made choices how to do life at the time (selling one's annoying brother)
> *Prescriptive* = command from God about how to live or do something that applies to all believers, all people groups, and all time periods (don't have sex with another person's spouse).

So, we can't take Genesis chapters 42-44 and create a formula for treating your estranged family members with God's blessing on the result. We don't know the reasons Joseph had for his actions. It is not a good idea to speculate because often your speculation becomes fact when it shouldn't be. We will look at what Joseph asked of his brothers and how they responded.

1. In Genesis 42:6-13, describe the encounter between Joseph and his brothers.

2. Joseph has learned much about managing people. He puts that to work in relating to his brothers. What does Joseph demand of his brothers (verses 14-20)?

3. What types of feelings do Joseph's actions awaken within his brothers (verses 21-22, 28)?

4. What is awakened in Joseph during this encounter?

5. Read Genesis 42:29-43:14. What grabbed your attention?

Leaving Simeon in custody in Egypt, Joseph's brothers return home to collect Benjamin. But, when they relate their startling news to Jacob, he refuses to release Benjamin. Only later, when they run out of food, does he let Benjamin go. So, Joseph's brothers, burdened with anxiety and bearing gifts, arrive in Egypt with Benjamin.

6. Read Genesis 43:15-34. Let's look at what happens.

    • How does Joseph receive them this time and why (vv. 16, 24-25)?

    • How does he react to the sight of Benjamin (v 30)?

    • What information is given in v. 32?

    • Compare Genesis v. 26 with 37:7-8. What is happening?

7. Discuss v. 23—what it says, who says it, and what it reveals about Joseph.

8. ***Your life's journey:*** We don't know who is listening or watching when we are going through difficult times. It's okay to be honest with our feelings. David told God and others whenever he was angry or hurting or disappointed. But, usually the very next sentences from his pen / mouth were praises for who God is and how God has helped him in the past. You see this in practically every psalm he wrote. What are you telling others as you are struggling? How can you communicate that God is good even in the tough times and that you can trust Him with what He chooses to do in your life?

Respond to the Lord about what He's shown you today.

Day Two Study

Read Genesis 44:1-34. Ask the Lord Jesus to teach you through His Word.

9. After they feast and are given grain, the bewildered men depart. But Joseph tests them one more time by putting his silver cup in Benjamin's sack then sending a servant after them to find it. Again, we don't know the reasons. But, we can look at what happened and the results. When Joseph's silver cup is found in Benjamin's sack, what was their reaction (vv.13-14)?

Historical Insight: Joseph told his servant in Genesis 44:5 to claim that the silver cup supposedly stolen was used for divination. Divination is the practice of using objects or people to uncover hidden knowledge, especially about the future. Since all Egyptian nobility at that time would have owned a silver divination cup, the most likely scenario is that Joseph did, too. But, Joseph had no need to use a cup for divination. God had enabled him to have prophetic dreams himself and to interpret the dreams of others. Joseph found his success in God without the use of props. So, the reference to divination may have been used to make the cup more valuable and, therefore, make the brothers feel guiltier for having it. Later, God forbid the use of divination for His people (Deuteronomy 18:10). Divination would include reading palms, tea leaves, tarot cards, star charts, or any kind of fortune telling. It is rebellion against God and seeking truth from evil spirits. (*Gotquestions.org*)

10. Joseph's words in v. 17 elicit a response from Judah (whose idea it was to sell Joseph into slavery). How does Judah respond (vv. 18-34)?

11. What does v. 34 especially demonstrate about Judah and his brothers?

12. **Your life's journey:** Joseph's patience with his brothers before revealing himself was certainly testing his character as well as that of his siblings. We can debate whether Joseph was right or not. Was it testing or revenge? Was it necessary? One thing we can know is that revenge has no place in the gospel or in a Christian's life. In the New Testament, we are told not to repay anyone evil for evil. Do not take revenge, but leave room for God to enact justice. And, He will do it. Justice will be done—whether in this life through the legal system or after death. But, for now, Jesus calls us as individual believers to respond differently. Read Romans 12:17-21.

- Instead of meeting evil with equal or greater force, what are we instructed to do?

- What would this look like in your life regarding someone who has hurt you?

Ask the Lord to help you with this. You can say, "Lord Jesus, I can't do this kind thing to that person on my own. But, you can do it in me and through me. I will trust you." Then, watch what He does!

Respond to the Lord about what He's shown you today.

DAY THREE STUDY

Read Genesis 45:1-46:4. Ask the Lord Jesus to teach you through His Word.

13. Let's look at this touching reunion of brothers after 22 years.

- What happened in 45:1-2?

- How do Joseph's brothers react to the news that this powerful Egyptian is really their brother, whom they mistreated and abused 22 years ago (v. 3)?

- How does Joseph reassure them (vv. 4-8)?

- What is Joseph's plan for his family (vv. 9-13)?

14. With Pharaoh's blessing, Joseph sends home provisions for all his family. The brothers relay the news to their father, Jacob. What is Jacob's response 45:25-46:1)?

15. What assurance does God give to Jacob that this is the right move to make (46:2-4)?

Joseph sends his brothers back to Canaan to bring their father and his household to Egypt (72 blood relatives plus lots of in-laws). Jacob, 130 years old by now, is brought to Egypt to be protected through the famine, living on the fertile land of Goshen granted to him by Pharaoh. Some of the brothers became administrators for Pharaoh. Joseph has an emotional reunion with his father (Genesis 46:28-30). On his deathbed (Genesis 49), Jacob prophesies over each of his sons who are the ancestors of the nation of Israel. These Hebrews could hardly have grown in such numbers in the open territory of Canaan as they did in Egypt. In a very real sense, Egypt was a womb in which the seed of Israel grew and multiplied until in God's own time a nation was born.

16. Read Genesis 50:15-22. Jacob dies. The brothers are afraid of Joseph. What is Joseph's *continual* attitude toward his brothers and everything that has happened to him?

17. How is such an attitude possible from someone who has experienced so much pain in his life? Think about what Joseph had learned.

> **Scriptural Insight:** God tells us in His Word that trouble is an everyday part of the human experience (Matthew 7:25). God also tells us that God can and will use each and every painful circumstance we experience in life to achieve a greater good (Romans 8:28). But when we are besieged with trouble, God's greater purpose may not be immediately obvious to us. For Joseph, it took 22 years of waiting and choosing to respond in faith on a daily basis before he could see God's greater purpose for the nation of Israel. Joseph's amazing attitude towards the tragic circumstances of his life is summed up in Genesis 50:20, "You meant it for evil against me, but God meant it for good."

18. Read Psalm 105:16-24. What further insight does this psalm give us about Joseph's life?

19. ***Your life's journey:*** During a time of trial, three things are often affected that one must deal with in some way. Place (moving to new surroundings, out of your comfort zone). Position (status change, family life, financial opportunities). Personal character (responding to the change, trial, challenge). We've seen Joseph taken from his home, sold into slavery, and taken to Egypt. But, God used that to preserve the lives of people during the famine. From position of favored son, Joseph became a prisoner, then eventually overseer of food for all of Egypt. Joseph persevered through that and could see the fruit of his perseverance as he functioned well through each phase. As a person, Joseph developed into a mature man of God. Read Romans 5:3-5. Joseph's life illustrates these truths.

Take some quiet time to reflect on a trial you have faced in the past or are facing right now. How have you been affected in place, position, and character? Where do you see the fruit of perseverance through that trial? Respond to the Lord using any creative element (prose poem, picture, song) to illustrate what God has taught you about resting in His promise to work things together for good in your life (Romans 8:28).

Recommended: *Listen to the podcast "God Works It for Good" after doing this lesson to reinforce what you have learned. Use the listener guide on the next page.*

God Works It for Good

MOVING BEYOND THE PAIN

- Joseph has learned much about managing people over the years. He puts that to work in relating to his brothers. We don't know the reasons Joseph had for the actions he took with them. Whatever his reasons, it gave him time to prepare his own heart so that he could respond rightly to them when he revealed himself.

- Joseph saw a greater purpose in the tragic circumstances of his life than just for himself. What his brothers did to him was horrible, evil. No doubt about it. But, Joseph had a choice. He could follow the pattern of anger, despair and self-pity. Or, he could trust God to do something on his behalf that would be good for him and bring God glory.

  "Don't be afraid. Am I in the place of God? As for you, you meant to harm me, but God intended it for a good purpose, so he could preserve the lives of many people, as you can see this day." (Genesis 50:20, NET)

- God "intended it for a good purpose." The Hebrew root word used there means "to weave together." God worked it together for a good purpose (Romans 8:28). The fact that God can work things together for good doesn't mean that those things are good.

- God's plan all along was to get Abraham's descendants to Egypt where they would live for 400 years (Genesis 15). God allowed Joseph's brothers to sell him into slavery. But, God didn't do the evil. The brothers did. God took that situation and Joseph's faith walk with Him and wove it to bring about His plan to save lives. God worked it for good. Just like a weaver does.

THE GIFT OF HUMAN FREEDOM ALLOWS FOR EVIL CHOICES

- Why does God let people do evil? Why doesn't He stop it if He is capable of doing so? The true answer to that is that God does stop evil all the time. Every day He stops evil.

- Why doesn't He stop all evil? To stop all evil would mean to stop all human freedom. God takes our freedom and responsibility more seriously than we do.

- We demand our freedom to do what we want to do. Then, when something bad happens, we blame God for letting it happen. God lets humans be free and responsible for what they do. We can't blame God for humans doing wrong.

- You don't have to have an answer for all bad things happening. In this world, all will not turn out well. When we are with Christ, we will have the whole story.

WHAT TO SAY AND NOT SAY WHEN EVIL THINGS HAPPEN

- **Caution #1:** Don't minimize the evil or the hurt. You can say to the victim of any violent incident, "That was terrible, and those people are responsible for what they did. But, God is bigger and greater. If you will trust Him, then one day, whether in this life or the next, you will see how He fulfilled that promise to work that bad thing into something good. You can respond by faith now when things aren't ideal, or you can keep being the bitter victim."

- **Caution #2:** Don't say, "I'm sure God has a plan or purpose for this." Instead, say this: "I don't know why things happen in the world. I do know that God is good, that He loves you, that you can go to Him for comfort, and He will strengthen and help you. I know He is not finished with you, and He has a future for you."

- **Caution #3:** Don't say, "God is in control." The truth is that God is sovereign over all of human history and what He allows or doesn't allow humans to do. But, the evil is still evil. God is not doing it. The key is to trust God whether you understand or not and to believe that God works it eventually for good for someone. It might not be just for you.

- **Caution #4:** Don't encourage revenge. Revenge has no place in the gospel or in a Christian's life. We are told not to repay anyone evil for evil, but leave room for God to enact justice. Justice will be done—whether in this life through the legal system or after death (Romans 12:20-21).

CONCLUSION

Here are 4 points to remember about this issue of God working all things for good:

- We live in a fallen, wicked, cursed world with suffering, evil and death. A broken world.

- God has chosen from the beginning to give human beings the freedom to act. When someone asks, "Why did this wicked thing happen?" Answer with, "An evil human being did this."

- God promises to accomplish a greater good in and for all people who trust in Him (8:29), conforming us to the image of His Son. Suffering is one of His tools to do that.

- We live in the last days of the old creation. Our great and powerful God will one day wrap up history and fix it. We live in the hope of this happening in our future.

To someone who is a casualty of this wicked world (cancer, death, rape, murder), try giving them this counsel: "I don't know if there is any answer to this. But, I do know that Jesus said, 'Come to Me, and I will give you rest.' If you go to Jesus Christ today, you will find comfort and rest from anxiety. The world is not always good, but God is always good. That's why you can trust Him."

We can have hope because we have God with us. So, remember our lane markers for the race.

#1. Choose to persevere through every challenge.
#2. Count on God's promise to give you hope.
#3. Let that hope sustain you through the rough-and-tumble of life.
#4. Celebrate the joyful reward.

Let Jesus satisfy your heart with hope so you can persevere through life.

David—The Man after God's Heart

5 A Heart of Hope
1 Samuel 16-22:2 and selected Psalms

For whatever was written in former days was written for our instruction, that through endurance and through the encouragement of the Scriptures we might have hope. (Romans 15:4, ESV)

DAY ONE STUDY—DAVID'S CALLING

Historical Perspective

After Moses and Joshua died, the people of Israel were governed by a series of judges and priests. This was an effective system only if the leaders and people were committed to following the Lord. The book of Judges in the Old Testament records the failure of this system because of the faithlessness of the Israelites. In the book of Deuteronomy, God had predicted this failure and knew that eventually Israel would be ruled by a king.

Around 1051 BC, the people of Israel demanded that the prophet Samuel select a king to rule over them. Samuel's sons were dishonest judges, not qualified for the job. God had predicted Israel's desire for a king so they could "be like other nations." However, God had called Israel to be unlike all other nations. In calling for a king, Israel was indirectly rejecting God as ruler. The Lord agreed to let the people have a king to rule them, thus Saul was chosen as the first king of Israel. Saul was a "choice and handsome man" and stood head and shoulders above all other men. Yet, he was impetuous, hot-tempered, disobedient and jealous. Saul was 30 years old when he became king (in 1050 BC) and reigned over Israel 42 years. After Saul openly disobeyed God twice, God told Saul that his kingdom would not endure and that God had sought out a man after his own heart. That man was David.

In our Bibles, more has been written about David (sixty-six chapters) than any other Old Testament character. We not only can read about David's life in 1 and 2 Samuel, 1 Kings and 1 Chronicles, we can glean insight into what he thought and felt by reading many of the Psalms he wrote (73 are attributed to David). In the New Testament, there are fifty-nine references to this great man.

In Hebrew, the name David means "beloved." David is the only person in the Bible whose epitaph reads "a man after God's own heart." David was born in 1040 BC and was the youngest son of Jesse. He is described as handsome and ruddy with beautiful eyes. He was anointed as a boy to be God's chosen king by the prophet Samuel and from that day forward, the Holy Spirit remained with him for the rest of his life.

In the Hebrew Bible, First and Second Samuel were originally one book called the Book of Samuel. The Greek Septuagint translation of the Old Testament (made ca. 250 B.C.) was the first to divide it into two books. Most conservative scholars think that Samuel may have written or been responsible for noting what is in 1 Samuel 1-24. Then some other writer(s), perhaps the prophets Gad and Nathan, finished the recording of events after Solomon's death.

Recommended: *Read or listen to 1 Samuel 16-31; all of 2 Samuel; and 1 Kings 1:1-2:12 to get the "Big Picture" of David's life as you do this study.*

---

1. ***Deeper Discoveries (optional):*** Find out more information about the time period in which David lived.

    - The process and meaning of anointing—

    - Meaning of "the kings table"—

    - The showbread—

    - The "ark of the covenant" and its significance—

Ask the Lord Jesus to teach you through His Word.

Most everyone who has ever been to Sunday school or Vacation Bible School as a child knows the familiar story of David and Goliath. The young shepherd boy slew the giant with one stone and a simple slingshot. We know that this brave shepherd boy grew up to be a great king of Israel. We also know that Jesus Christ descended from the house of David. Who was this David, and what can we learn from him?

2. Read the following verses that give us a descriptive picture of David. From these, we get insight into what God saw in David's personality and character. What do you learn?

    - 1 Samuel 13:13-14—

    - 1 Samuel 16:5-13, 18—

    - 1 Samuel 17:26, 32-37, 45-47—

Historical Insight: I wonder how many people think that David, after he killed the giant, within a matter of just a few days took the throne and became the youngest king in the history of Israel? Well, in case you were one who thought that, you need to know it didn't happen that way. (Charles Swindoll, *David*, p. 51)

David was about 16 when he was anointed by Samuel and 30 when he became king over Judah.

3. Read 1 Samuel 16:14-23 and 17:15. David was anointed to become king and now knew that God had something more for him than tending sheep the rest of his life. He just didn't know the "when." Initially, as David waited patiently on God's timing and direction, what was he doing?

Scriptural Insight from 1 Samuel 16:14-15: The Spirit of God not only departed from Saul, but God permitted an evil spirit to "torment" Saul as judgment for Saul's sins. Saul was then left to rule in his own strength without the Holy Spirit to help him. Note that the Spirit of the Lord departs from Saul before an evil spirit came. Before Pentecost (Acts 2), the Holy Spirit never permanently resided on anyone except for David (1 Samuel 16:13) and John the Baptist (Luke 1:15, 41). The Spirit of God would come for a temporary time to enable someone for an act of service to God and then depart (and then possibly come again for another act of service). The absence or presence of the Holy Spirit in the Old Testament says nothing about salvation. However, at Pentecost, and to the present era, the Holy Spirit comes into the believer at the moment of salvation and seals us until the day of redemption (Ephesians 4:30). He will NEVER, EVER depart from us!

4. What does this show you about David's character even as a teen?

5. *Your life's journey:* Have you ever been in a position where you knew God was leading you in a certain direction, yet the timing wasn't right? Describe how you knew the timing was not right and what you did in the waiting.

Respond to the Lord about what He's shown you today.

DAY TWO STUDY—DAVID'S CHALLENGES

Ask the Lord Jesus to teach you through His Word.

6. Read 1 Samuel 18-19:2. After David's valiant defeat over Goliath (chapter 17), he remained in Saul's service. What were some of David's life challenges and rewards in this time of his life?

7. Like Joseph, David was treated unfairly by others. It would have been easy for David to feel deserted by God and alone. But what was really happening (1 Samuel 18:5,12,14,28,30)?

Think About It: Joseph waited 13 years before he knew his purpose for being in Egypt. David was told his purpose at the beginning then had to wait for it to become reality.

Though Jonathan reminds his father that David has been loyal and that his deeds have benefited Saul greatly, Saul does not listen. He became more and more jealous of David and doubles his efforts to kill David. David must escape. Let's look at whom God used to help David and how they did it.

8. Read 1 Samuel 19:1-24.

- Who helped David and how (vv. 11-13)?

- What did God do in vv. 18-24 to stop Saul?

Think About It: Whom has God sent to help you when you were in a time of danger or distress?

9. Read 1 Samuel 20:30-42. Who helped David and how?

David, the boy anointed by God as the next king of Israel was now on the run from a madman. The bottom had seemingly dropped out of David's life, yet he persevered despite hopeless circumstances. Though God had provided a means for escape, every tangible support system in David's life had been removed one by one until he had nothing left to lean on except God. All his "props" of normal life were removed. Yet, David had hope in *"the God who fulfills His purpose for me"* as expressed in Psalm 57:2.

10. *Your life's journey:* I know I would discover some ugliness about myself should all my "props of normal life" be removed. But, I know there is some ugliness right now with all my props still in place. My joyful walk should not be dependent on my props. My trust in God's love and goodness to me should not be dependent on my props. Your trust in God and joyful life in Him doesn't need to depend on your props, either.

Have you thought about what would be left if all your "props" were removed? How would you react? Maybe this has already happened to you so you know the answer. What can you learn from the examples of both David and Joseph to help you continue to function well?

Respond to the Lord about what He's shown you today.

DAY THREE STUDY—DAVID'S HOPE

We can read the facts about what happened to David while he was "on the run." But, we also have the great blessing of reading his journal. The psalms David wrote during that time are like a journal revealing what David was thinking and feeling during his years of flight from Saul. Since they are Scripture, the truths expressed in them are for us to know and apply as well.

Ask the Lord Jesus to teach you through His Word.

11. Read 1 Samuel 21:1-15. David is now homeless and alone. He's desperate. What was provided to help David (vv. 1-9)?

12. David wrote 2 psalms during his time in Gath.

    Read Psalm 34:1-9.

    - What is he feeling and doing?

    - What does he remember about God (vv. 6, 8-9)?

    Read Psalm 56:1-13.

    - Psalm 56:3-4 are key verses for us to remember whenever we are afraid. Write them in the space below.

13. God answers David's prayers in several ways. Read 1 Samuel 22:1-5.

    - How does God provide for David's aloneness?

    - How does God provide safety for David's parents?

    - How does God give David direction of where to go?

14. Saul learns of the High Priest's assistance given to David and kills all the priests. David is distraught about this news.

    Read Psalm 52:1-9.

    - What is he feeling and doing?

    - What does he remember about God?

    - How will he respond to God's faithfulness?

15. David was now living in a remote valley with 400 malcontents (those who were evading over-taxation by Saul or who were discontented with how Saul had treated them). What could have been David's reaction towards God if David had focused on outward circumstances?

Think About It: Oswald Chambers (20th century author) said this, "If God allows you to be stripped of the exterior portions of your life, he means for you to cultivate the interior." Someone described this as a spiritual maturity gym where you need to complete the whole circuit to gain the desired results. As we saw in Joseph's life, David trusted God and took the next step to function well.

You can look at the map below to get an idea of how much "on the run" David was for the better part of 13 years.

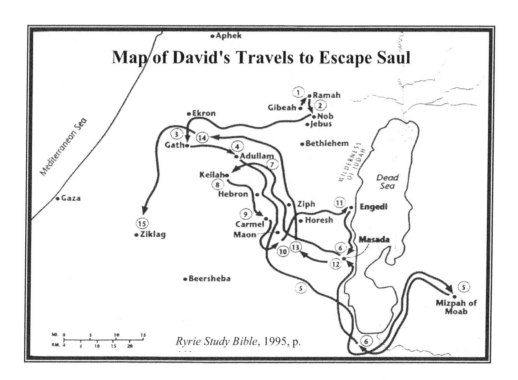

Map of David's Travels to Escape Saul

Ryrie Study Bible, 1995, p.

Focus on the Meaning: Waiting (especially in the Bible) is the rule rather than the exception. So, we had better learn how to deal with it and still grow as we go through it. By definition, waiting implies readiness, something you expect and hope. It doesn't imply inactivity, passivity or stagnation. (Lori Schweers)

16. David understood waiting on God. If we live by David's example, we need to learn how to wait (to be patient) on God's perfect timing. God is in the "human development business." What can we know for sure while we wait?

- Philippians 1:6 —

- 1 Thessalonians 5:24 —

- Ephesians 2:10 —

    From the Greek: The Greek word for patience (one definition) is *hypomone*. It is defined as the "quality of endurance under trials. Those possessing this virtue are free from cowardice or discouragement. It is mainly an attitude of the heart with respect to things [or circumstances]." (Adapted from *The NIV Compact Dictionary of the Bible,* by J.D. Douglas and Merrill C. Tenney)

17. ***Your life's journey:*** While David was waiting on God, he was expressing to God his fears and anger and distress. He was crying out to God and asking for deliverance and guidance. He was remembering what he knew to be true about God and what God had done for him in the past. How does David's example of patiently waiting on God encourage you to wait on God in whatever circumstances you find yourself?

Respond to the Lord about what He's shown you today.

Recommended: *Listen to the podcast "Loyalty Affects How You Approach Life" after doing this lesson to reinforce what you have learned. Use the listener guide on the next page.*

Loyalty Affects How You Approach Life

Loyalty is "the quality of devotion or attachment to somebody or something." It's both a feeling and an action. Some of us by nature tend to be loyal. Others of us are more skeptical, maybe preferring to be mavericks out on our own. Loyalty is being tested every day in homes and businesses and human relationships across this planet. Who demands your loyalty? Who has the right to it? Do they receive it from you? How good are you at remaining loyal? Loyalty affects how you approach life. And, for every believer who calls herself a Christian, Jesus deserves your loyalty.

JESUS DESERVES YOUR LOYALTY

- The moment you trust in Jesus Christ as your savior, you get a new life fused together with His and a new identity. You are now said to be in Christ, a Child of God, one of God's saints, totally accepted and loved by Him.

- You are set free to live a radically different kind of life. And, in that freedom, you have a choice. Who are you going to serve with your life now? God or yourself? The best choice to make is saying to Jesus, "I am YOUR woman forever. I serve you."

- **How** do we do that with all the distractions around us? By that, I don't mean our families or jobs. Serving them well is serving Jesus loyally. I mean, all the other ways of approaching life. All of those voices calling out to us from our culture. How do we remain loyal to Jesus as our master and His way of approaching life?

- We can loyally serve Jesus through humility and obedience. Loyalty requires humility. And, humility leads to obedience. Both of those offer a reward.

LOYALTY REQUIRES HUMILITY

- In the New Testament, humility means "lowliness of mind." It is how you think of yourself. But, it's not feeling low or down or depressed. Instead, it pictures a servant bowing before a master.

- Jesus' invitation to us in Matthew 11:28-29 puts together two words that are related—gentle and humble. He uses them to describe himself. In Ephesians 4:1-2, Paul puts these same two words together to describe how we are to live as believers. Gentleness in the Bible carries the idea of strength under control. It is the outworking of humility and a work of the Holy Spirit.

- You choose humility before God by recognizing His authority over you. You know that you've made that decision when you are willing to trust in God's goodness and accept His dealings with you as good without fighting Him on it. Then that choice is reflected in your gentle behavior towards others.

- Humility is the opposite of self-assertiveness and self-interest. It is recognizing that you do some things well because God gave you the genetics, intelligence, and opportunity to do so. And, you give Him the credit for it.

HUMILITY LEADS TO OBEDIENCE

- What good is a servant who refuses to obey? Or, who is out there trumpeting herself and her own will, and occasionally remembering to do what Jesus wants?

  God would rather I have understanding of 2 verses that I obey immediately than 20 verses that I don't. **Obedience is the key to discernment. It's not "capture and remember;" it's "hear and obey."** (Chip Ingram, DTS Leader Board)

- It's obedience to God's will for us revealed in His Word that grows us to maturity. Humility before God means you have already got obeying God settled in your mind. Now, you can obey Him in the rest of what He desires for your life to please Him.

- What are some hindrances to our obedience? One is lack of understanding of God's commands. Another hindrance is selectively choosing what we will obey. That leads us to being what the Bible describes as weak-willed women, always learning but never able to recognize truth for what it really is (2 Timothy 3:6). Lack of seeing the ugliness of our sin also hinders obedience. Obedience is necessary to remain loyal to Jesus and not get carried away by sin and all those other ways of approaching life.

OBEDIENCE OFFERS PROTECTION

- Obedience is necessary to protect yourself from those who distort the truth and draw you away from Jesus and His way of approaching life. *Acts 20:28-31*

- When you humble yourself before Jesus as your master and choose to obey His commands revealed to you in the Bible, you will be able to recognize truth from anything that is distorted. But, when you resist the discipline that comes from obedience, you are vulnerable to embracing whatever new heresy comes along as a fad. And, you cannot recognize the truth when you see it.

Loyalty affects how you approach life—Jesus' way or all those other options out there that offer nothing lasting. Jesus as Lord deserves our loyalty. Loyalty requires humility. Humility leads to obedience. Obedience offers protection from being sucked into every new fad that comes along. Have you already made that decision to say, "Lord Jesus, I am YOUR woman every day?" If not, will you do that today?

We can have hope because we have God with us. So, remember our lane markers for the race.

- #1. Choose to persevere through every challenge.
- #2. Count on God's promise to give you hope.
- #3. Let that hope sustain you through the rough-and-tumble of life.
- #4. Celebrate the joyful reward.

Let Jesus satisfy your heart with hope so you can persevere through life.

David—The Man after God's Heart

6 A Heart Open to Instruction
1 Samuel 23-26

Such things were written in the Scriptures long ago to teach us. And the Scriptures give us hope and encouragement as we wait patiently for God's promises to be fulfilled. (Romans 15:4, NLT)

DAY ONE STUDY

Historical Perspective

As a young boy, David tended his father's sheep. While in his teens, he gained national attention by killing Goliath, the Philistine giant from Gath. He was employed by King Saul to periodically appear in his palace to soothe him with his skillful harp playing. During this time, Saul's son, Jonathan, became David's closest friend. Because of David's continual military victories, Saul became exceedingly jealous over David's popularity. Saul openly sought to kill David, thus began a thirteen-year period of time that David was forced to flee from Saul.

We now find David and his band of 600 men living in the wilderness, in the "strongholds" of Engedi. (See map in the previous lesson.) Engedi is east of Hebron on the shores of the Dead Sea. It was marked by many caves in limestone cliffs, lush vegetation, fresh water springs and waterfalls. The caves were a natural refuge and provided a lookout spot from which to see an enemy approaching. From what we learned in our last lesson, we know that Saul was committed to killing David and was still pursuing him ardently.

1. ***Deeper Discoveries (optional):*** Find out more information about the Philistines and why they were enemies of God and Israel.

Read 1 Samuel 23:1-19. Ask the Lord Jesus to teach you through His Word.

> **Scriptural Insight:** 1 Samuel 23:6 says the High Priest Abiathar "brought the ephod with him." In it were two stones or similar objects, known as the Urim ("lights") and Thummim ("perfections"). One was light; the other was dark in color. The high priest carried them in the pocket on the front of his ephod (apron). We assume that a meaning was assigned to each (yes/no and true/false). The High Priest ascertained God's will by drawing or tossing one out. No one knows exactly what they were or how they were used. The Bible simply does not give us enough information.

2. What did David consistently do to get direction from God (vv. 2, 4, 10, 12)?

3. What did David do with the direction given by the Lord?

4. The Ziphites (second half of this passage and in chapter 26) said they would help Saul trap David. David wrote a psalm after finding out about this. Read Psalm 54.

   • What was David feeling and doing?

   • What was David remembering about God?

   • How will he respond to God's faithfulness?

5. *Your life's journey:* In 1 Samuel 13, you can read how Saul only partially obeyed God's direction and then justified his choice and behavior as being just as good. His idea was better in his own mind.

   • How are you at obeying the word of the Lord already given to you in the Bible? Are there parts that you twist to sound better in your own mind?

   • Or, how are you like David, willing to obey God's written word even if you don't totally understand why?

Respond to the Lord about what He's shown you today.

DAY TWO STUDY

Read 1 Samuel 24. As the Lord Jesus to teach you through His Word.

6. Focus on vv. 1-7.

    • What is happening in verses 1-3?

    • What did David's men (numbering ~600) encourage David to now do?

    • What did David choose to do, and how did he respond to his men?

    • What prevented David from seizing the moment and killing Saul?

    Think About It: David was able to restrain himself from killing Saul, but he couldn't resist the temptation to cut off some of his robe. We often do the same to those who have hurt us with a little cut here or a little jab there. Cutting off Saul's robe may have felt good at the moment, but it didn't mend David's injury. Healing came for David when he confronted Saul with the truth.

7. David knew that he had been anointed for a special purpose. It seemed obvious to everyone that he would be the next king. This was a golden opportunity to kill Saul and take the throne as the rightful leader. Christ was similarly tempted in the wilderness. Read Matthew 4:8-10. How are these situations similar?

    Think About It: The Bible is a real book, and this unique story is living proof. In the midst of his mad rush for vengeance, Saul must answer the call of nature. So, he finds himself crouching in the privacy of a cave – but not just any cave. He tromps right into the mouth of the cave where David and his men were hiding. Talk about being vulnerable! Bad enough for the king to be seen at that moment, but to be in the very presence of the enemy. Oh, man! (Charles Swindoll, *David*, p. 84)

8. Focus on vv. 8-22. David risked his life by revealing himself to Saul.

- Basically, what does David say to Saul? Why?

- How does Saul react to David?

- Considering human nature, what impact could this have had on David's men who were watching?

Scriptural Insight: The desire for vengeance or revenge can be one of life's most subtle temptations. We may suffer a personal injury, and we wait for just the right opportunity to repay the offending party. Whatever we call it, God calls it revenge. And, as we learned in Joseph's life, God is our avenger (Romans 12:17-21-13:4). He uses governmental authority to avenge evil and protect the good. He also intervenes in personal situations. While waiting, we are His agents of kindness, truth, and love as David did here. Since we are not all-seeing and all-wise, it's best to leave vengeance in the hands of our just and holy God.

9. Saul reneged on his promise and went after David again. Read 1 Samuel 26:5-12. Abishai (David's nephew) wants David to let him spear Saul.

- How does David respond this time?

- What did Abishai miss from David's last close encounter with Saul (1 Samuel 24)?

10. Read Psalm 57, written during this time.

- How is David trusting God?

- How is he praising God?

> **Recommended:** Search "Be exalted O God above the heavens" on YouTube to listen to a beautiful praise chorus based on this psalm.

11. *Your life's journey:*

- In what ways does David's honest confrontation with Saul give you a positive example of how to deal with someone who has wronged you?

- If a confrontation is not possible, what can you do to bring closure to a painful situation? Read Colossians 3:12-13 to see God's way of approaching this.

Respond to the Lord about what He's shown you today.

DAY THREE STUDY

This chapter includes 2 losses for David. One was the death of Israel's last judge and David's mentor, Samuel (v. 1). The other is David's wife, Michal, being given to another man by Saul (v. 44). After resisting the temptation to kill Saul and get on with his own kingship, David and his men moved on to the wilderness of Maon, a desert area 8 miles south of Hebron. There, they protected the shepherds who watched over Nabal's flocks. According to the customs of the day, during sheep shearing time the rancher would set aside a portion of the profits and give it to those who had protected his shepherds. This was, in a sense, a gratuity, just as we tip a waiter for good service. The tradition was not a law but an implied contract.

Read 1 Samuel 25:1-44. Ask the Lord Jesus to teach you through His Word.

12. Describe Nabal and Abigail.

- Nabal—

- Abigail—

13. Each character in the story makes a choice amidst the many conflicts and personal agendas.

- What choices did Nabal make?

- What choices did Abigail make?

- What choices did David make?

14. Throughout the conflict God was at work in the situation.

    - How was God faithful to Abigail?

    - How was God faithful to David?

    Think About It: Consider how such a rash action as David was about to undertake would have affected his men and his reputation. Abigail's words to David appeal to this consequence as motivation to stop his plan.

15. ***Your life's journey:*** In the first half of this lesson we find David immediately responsive to God's Holy Spirit (1 Samuel 24:5). However, his quick temper reduced him to initially responding in the flesh (i.e., fallen human nature) to Nabal's selfishness. How can this be?!

    - Paul experienced the same conflict. Read Romans 7:15-25. Can you relate?

    - How then can we live victoriously in this life we live on earth? Is it possible? Read John 15:5; Galatians 2:20 and Galatians 5:16 for insight.

16. ***Your life's journey:*** Throughout this study of David so far, you have seen how David illustrated for us the necessity of being open to godly instruction or advice and closed-minded to bad (worldly) instruction or advice. David needed to listen to and heed the instruction from Jonathan (1 Samuel 20), from the prophet Gad (1 Samuel 22), from God through all the inquiries he made (1 Samuel 21, 23), and now with Abigail. Being able to detect godly advice from worldly advice is called discernment.

    - How are you doing at discerning the difference between godly advice and worldly advice?

- Read Philippians 1:9-11. Being able to discern good from bad is a work of the Spirit in our lives. You can ask for this. Just say, "Lord Jesus, I can't do this on my own. I ask you to help me to discern good from bad so that I can act with godliness and glorify you. I trust you to do this in me and through me." Then, watch what He does!

Respond to the Lord about what He's shown you today.

Recommended: *Listen to the podcast "The Strong Support of Friends as You Persevere" after doing this lesson to reinforce what you have learned. Use the listener guide on the next page.*

The Strong Support of Friends as You Persevere

After being anointed as Israel's future king, David spent the next couple of years going back and forth between playing music for Saul and tending his father's sheep. Then, King Saul becomes exceedingly jealous over David's success and begins a long campaign to wipe out David. David soon finds himself on the run without any familiar comforts. All of his props of normal life were removed. Props are those things in life that give us support and take care of our needs.

WHAT'S LEFT WHEN OUR PROPS ARE REMOVED?

- The story of Martin and Gracia Burnham. After her props were removed, she realized that all she really had were her relationship with her God and her character to deal with the situation.

- Consider the props of normal life for you. What would you be like if all your props were removed?

- David had all his props removed. His journal psalms reveal how he felt at the time. Yet, he continued to trust in his God along the way. And, God sent to him a gift of new props, even in the wilderness.

THE STRONG SUPPORT OF FRIENDS

- God gave David the gift of a friend—Saul's son Jonathan. Jonathan warned David when Saul was on the warpath against him. Jonathan sacrificed his own time with David when he gave the message that David had to leave the king's house. When David was hiding in the wilderness, Jonathan came and encouraged him in the Lord.

- Not only Jonathan, but God also sent his prophets to give David direction about where to go next.

- David's family came to him in the cave to be with him. But, then he had to hide his parents from Saul, too, by taking them to Moab.

- Then, God sent strong, noble, and faithful men to surround David. "David's Mighty Men" 1 Samuel 22:2; 1 Chronicles 11-12

    "We are yours, O David! We are with you, O son of Jesse! Success, success to you, and success to those who help you, for your God will help you." (1 Chronicles 12:18)

- If you are surrounded by godly people whom God sends to surround you, that is in a sense being supported by the army of God. God works through people to support us. He gives people to be our props.

- God does not intend for us to live life alone. So, surround yourself with other Christians who love the Lord. When a crisis hits, don't quit church, don't quit Bible studies, or don't quit fellowshipping with your small group. Don't pull back from the support God can give to you through people. Share your need with those who love the Lord and who will put a skip in your step with encouragement and support. Allow God to bless you through them.

- Avoid anyone who uses you up or encourages complaining or anger against God. That kind of person just sucks the joy right out of you.

- If you are a leader of a work team, a family, or a small group, make sure to ask God to surround you with people who will give your leadership strong support like David's "Mighty Men" did.

We can have hope because we have God with us. So, remember our lane markers for the race.

#1. Choose to persevere through every challenge.
#2. Count on God's promise to give you hope.
#3. Let that hope sustain you through the rough-and-tumble of life.
#4. Celebrate the joyful reward.

Let Jesus satisfy your heart with hope so you can persevere through life.

David—The Man after God's Heart

7 A Humble Heart

2 Samuel 7, 9, & 12

For whatever things were written before were written for our learning, that we through the perseverance and comfort of the Scriptures might have hope. (Romans 15:4, NKJV)

DAY ONE STUDY

Historical Perspective

Saul tried three times to seize and kill David, but was not successful. In 1 Samuel 31, we find Saul and his three sons killed on the battlefield. Second Samuel opens with David receiving the news of the deaths and mourning the loss, especially the loss of his dear friend, Jonathan. David waits for God's direction as to where to go next. God then tells David to go to Hebron where he is made king over the house of Judah. Seven and a half years later, after the death of Saul's son Ish-Bosheth, David was made king over all of Israel. Twenty years after he was taken out of the sheep pastures and anointed by Samuel, David became king over the whole nation (age 37-38).

Since the days of Joshua, the people of Israel had thought more in terms of *tribal* identity rather than *national* identity. David was successful in unifying Israel and Judah (the two main factions) by centralizing the government in Jerusalem, which he captured and made the capital city. Jerusalem was a wise choice politically and served to create harmony and unity between the two factions.

Through David, Jerusalem also became the center of worship for the Israelites when the Ark and what remained of the tabernacle was moved there. From that time on, Israel offered sacrifices only at Jerusalem and celebrated three special religious festivals there each year. From 1002 to 995 BC, David expanded his kingdom on all sides, and rest from war followed. Though David did not build the temple, he designed it (based on God's plan given to him) and made elaborate preparations for his son Solomon to build it.

Read 2 Samuel 7:1-29. Ask the Lord Jesus to teach you through His Word.

This occurred around 995 BC, around 15 years after David became king.

1. Focus on vv. 1-17.

   • What is in David's heart, and how does he approach the Lord about it?

   • What is God's answer to him about building the temple?

   • What is God's promise to him about the throne of his kingdom (dynasty)?

Scriptural Insight: God promises David His steadfast love as well as fatherly discipline to his heirs. We can see the fulfillment of God's promise to David when we look at the genealogy of Christ through Joseph in Matthew 1:1-17 (v. 6 refers to David) and the genealogy of Christ through Mary in Luke 3:23-38 (v. 31 refers to David in this line-up). God fulfills His promise to David in both Mary and Joseph. God is faithful and keeps His promises!

2. Focus on David's response to God in vv. 18-29. David responds to God with humility and gratitude.

   • What words show his humility?

   • What words show his gratitude?

Read 2 Samuel 9:1-13.

In ancient times, the family members of a previous king were often exterminated once the new dynasty took control in order to prevent them from trying to come back into power. Therefore, all family members of the prior dynasty had reason to live in fear once the new king took the throne. Saul's one remaining heir, Jonathan's son Mephibosheth, had been injured as a child and lived the rest of his life lame in both feet. Technically, Mephibosheth was the presumptive heir to the throne as the last living relative of Saul.

3. What kindness does David show to Jonathan's one remaining son?

   Focus on the Meaning: David's use of kindness is like saying, "I want to demonstrate the same kind of GRACE (loyal love) that God has demonstrated to me." It's interesting to note that David does not ask if anyone is deserving or qualified for this grace. He offers it unconditionally. David gives Mephibosheth an undeserved grace offering (vv. 9-10) and makes him part of his household so that he would eat at the king's table.

4. What do you learn about David as a man after God's own heart from both 2 Samuel 7 and 2 Samuel 9?

What David did for Mephibosheth, God does for us by His grace.

- When we come to Christ at salvation we are crippled by sin (Romans 5:6).

- Like David pursuing Mephibosheth, God is ardently pursuing us so He can extend to us His glorious grace (Luke 19:10).

- Like poor Mephibosheth, we have nothing to offer God for His priceless gift of grace. We can only humbly accept that which we don't deserve and could never deserve (Titus 3:5a).

- God can rescue us from our own personal "Lo-debar" of death and bring us to His house of grace. Colossians 1:21-22

- Just as Mephibosheth was adopted as a son and made royalty and ate at the king's table, we are adopted as royal daughters with all the rights and privileges of royalty in God's house (Galatians 4:7).

- Mephibosheth's limp was a constant reminder of his imperfections and of David's grace. Our imperfect state reminds us that where sin abounds, the grace of God super abounds (Romans 5:20b)

5. **Your life's journey:** If you have trusted in Christ, then like Mephibosheth you have been called, found and rescued. Through faith in Jesus, you have a place in God's house of grace. Respond to God in the space below using any creative means (poem, prayer, art, song) to express your humility and gratitude to Him.

Day Two Study

David the shepherd boy, the skilled musician, the valiant giant slayer, the successful military leader is given the throne over all of Israel. He takes a nation that has bottomed out spiritually, militarily and economically and binds it back together. He expands its boundaries from 6000-60,000 square miles. He establishes trade routes with the world. He builds up a mighty military force. He centralizes worship in Jerusalem. He is a national hero. What a courageous, faithful man after God's own heart UNTIL you get to 2 Samuel 11. The Bible paints a very clear picture of God's hatred for sin and the sad consequences David must face as he endures many family crises resulting from his sinful choices.

In looking at this low point in his life, we wonder how God could possibly call David "a man after God's own heart." The answer comes not in looking at David's personal successes or spiritual failures but in looking at David's *responsiveness to the Holy Spirit* (as we saw in the last lesson) and to his *teachable heart*.

6. ***Deeper Discoveries (optional):*** Find out more information about bathing and hygiene practices in the time period in which David lived.

Synopsis of what happened with David and Bathsheba (2 Samuel 11):

About 3 years after God's promise to establish David's throne in 2 Samuel 7 (~992 BC), David sees a young woman named Bathsheba bathing and lusts after her. Bathsheba's grandfather was one of David's counselors. Her father was one of David's bodyguards. She was married to a Gentile, one of David's royal guards, who must have adopted Israelite customs. Bathsheba likely grew up around the royal court so familiarity plays a role in this incident. The Bible does not call this incident rape as it does in other situations (2 Samuel 13:14). Bathsheba succumbed to David's advances. She is comfortable enough with David to send him word that she is pregnant, expecting him to do something to rescue her. David calls Uriah home from the battle for some R&R, but Uriah's honor as a soldier leads him to refuse to enjoy that time with his wife when his fellow soldiers are in danger. So, David hatches a plan with his general Joab to put Uriah on the front lines so that he would be killed. There you go.

Read 2 Samuel 11:27-12:25. Ask the Lord Jesus to teach you through His Word.

7. Focus on vv. 7-10. The prophet, Nathan, comes to David with a parable representing David's sinful deeds. How does God view David's actions?

Scriptural Insight: The author [of 2 Samuel] points his accusing finger at David, not Bathsheba. It was not Bathsheba's indiscretion in bathing herself, for she was simply obeying the ritual of purification outlined in the law—in the evening when the sun is setting. It is nearly dark. It was David who, by means of his lofty elevation and view, looked inappropriately at Bathsheba, violating her privacy. The sequence of sin in David's life does not end with his adulterous union with Bathsheba. It leads to a deceptive plot to make her husband Uriah appear to be the father of David's child with Bathsheba and culminates in David's murder of Uriah and his marriage to Uriah's wife, Bathsheba. (Bob Deffinbaugh, "David and Uriah," Bible.org)

8. Focus on vv. 10-14.

    • What does God (through Nathan) say is going to happen as a result of David's sin?

    Scriptural Insight: This is a rare explanation in Scripture as to why this baby died. Remember the difference between descriptive and prescriptive. We cannot use this verse to explain why other babies die. God has not given that as a law of cause and effect.

    • How does David react?

    • Instead of David's contrite (repentant) response, how could he have responded? Recall Saul's response in 1 Samuel 15 when confronted by the prophet Samuel. See also Proverbs 19:3.

    Historical Insight: God never lies. All that He said through Nathan came to pass. We can trace the line of David's sin with Bathsheba to eight consequences that led him on a downward path of grief and heartache.
    • David and Bathsheba's newborn son dies. (2 Samuel 12:14-18a)
    • David's son, Amnon, rapes his half-sister, Tamar. (2 Samuel 13:1-21)
    • David's son, Absalom, hates Amnon. (2 Samuel 13:22)
    • Absalom murders Amnon. (2 Samuel 13:28-29)
    • Absalom rebels and runs away. (2 Samuel 13:37-39)
    • Absalom leads a conspiracy. (2 Samuel 14:1-24)
    • Absalom violates David's wives. (2 Samuel 16:22)
    • Joab, David's general (& nephew), murders Absalom. (2 Samuel 18:14 & 33)
    (Adapted from Charles Swindoll, *David*, Bible study guide)

Keep in mind that David lived under the Mosaic Law. God judged David for his behavior and pronounced him guilty. As king, David had great accountability for his actions. Since he was anointed by God, his reputation reflected on God. Therefore, for the sake of God's holy reputation among the nations, David's sin of adultery and murder had to be judged (2 Samuel 12:14)

9. According to the Law, David deserved death for adultery with a married woman (Leviticus 20:10) and for murder of Uriah (Leviticus 24:17). However, God does not permit it. God extended His grace to David.

    - What did God say (v. 13)?

    - What does this tell you about God? See also Nehemiah 9:31; Exodus 33:19.

10. Focus on vv. 16-25. One of the best illustrations of living through the consequences of deliberate sin is found in the life of David. Let's examine David's response to the situation.

    - What was the first thing that David did when the baby became ill?

    - Where was David's focus?

    - When the child died, what did David do?

Focus on the Meaning: Life after death was something that was absolutely certain to David. David wasn't simply saying that he would join his child in death, he was anticipating a joyful reunion with this seven-day-old boy. For David, that could only be in heaven. And, so he worshiped God. David had great assurance that this little baby was in heaven and one day he would see that baby again. Later, in 2 Samuel 18, his grief over Absalom's death indicates his lack of assurance at seeing this son again after death. Second Samuel 12 is one of those passages that help us to understand that when little children die, God's character is such that He will make provision for them and we'll see them again in heaven someday. Based on the authority of Matt 19:13-14 and 2 Sam. 12:19-23, when an infant or small child dies, he or she slips into the Lord's presence instantly. How that child is dealt with or what happens so that he or she can enjoy heaven is not revealed for us. Apparently, God gives instant maturity and the ability to enjoy the things of heaven with the adults. But, I take it from verse 23 that the child is securely in the Lord's presence at the time of death. (Chuck Swindoll, *Insight for Living*)

11. How did God show His goodness to both David & Bathsheba after the baby died (vv. 24-25)?

Think About It: Does it amaze you that God would send a special word of love for this second child of David with Bathsheba? He also chose Solomon (who was down in the list of potential heirs) to be next in line for the throne after David. That's GRACE! Bathsheba joined two other women with marred reputations, Tamar and Rahab, in the genealogy of Jesus Christ (Matthew 1: 6-17).

12. ***Deeper Discoveries (optional):*** David was a powerful king of a large territory with much wealth and success. People follow their leaders. In such a tragic, emotional circumstance how could David have reacted? Look at 2 Chronicles 16:7-10; 26:16-20; 32:24-26; and 33:10-13 to see how his successors reacted to God's rebuke for their sin.

13. ***Your life's journey:*** Read the following quote then respond below.

> **Think About It:** In the company of David, we find someone who does it as badly as, or worse than, we do, but who in the process doesn't quit, doesn't withdraw from God. David's isn't an ideal life, but an actual life. We read David to cultivate a sense of reality for a true life, an honest life, a God-aware and God-responsive life. (Eugene Peterson, *Leap Over a Wall,* p. 62)

How do you respond to God when you don't get your way? In what way is your life an honest life, a God-aware and God-responsive life?

Respond to the Lord about what He's shown you today.

DAY THREE STUDY

Read Psalm 51 and 32. Ask the Lord Jesus to teach through His Word.

Psalms 51 and 32 are emotionally descriptive psalms written by David during this time in his life. They are his journals of what he was thinking and feeling and doing. In Psalm 51, you saw how David confessed his guilt and asked for forgiveness. In Psalm 32, David described the blessing of forgiveness as well as being cleansed of his guilt. Confessing our sins to our heavenly Father (which is *simply agreeing with God about the truth that you have sinned*) is oftentimes easier than accepting His *unconditional* forgiveness. We often believe we are forgiven but hang on to the guilt. Satan uses guilt to render us useless.

As a New Testament believer, God has declared us "not guilty" based on Jesus Christ's *finished* work on the cross. Where the Law offered a temporary "covering" for sins, Jesus Christ became *"the Lamb of God, who **takes away** the sin of the world" (John 1:29)*. While *"the blood of bulls and goats cannot take away sins" (Heb. 10:4)*, now *"by one offering [Christ] he has **perfected for all time** those who are made holy" (Heb. 10:14)*. The Christian has the blessing and privilege of rejoicing in the fullness of acceptance accomplished for us by our Savior Jesus Christ who bore our sins (past, present and future sins) as well as God's judgment on those sins. We who are in Christ will never have to worry about punishment or judgment (Romans 8:1 & Colossians 2:13-14.)

> **Scriptural Insight:** David prays after his sin with Bathsheba, *"Do not reject me! Do not take your Holy Spirit away from me!" (Psalm 51:11)*. Do Christians need to fear that God will withdraw His Spirit from them because of sin? No. The ministry of the Holy Spirit in Old Testament times was different. Today, every Christian receives the *permanent* indwelling of the Holy Spirit at the moment he or she trusts in Jesus Christ. Before Christ came, however, the Holy Spirit came only upon *certain* individuals to empower them for special service (such as prophets or kings), and there was no promise of permanence. In that psalm, David is actually praying that God will not take away his anointed role as king of Israel as He actually had done to the previous king, Saul (1 Samuel 16:14). While disobedient Christians may face temporal consequences or the discipline of God because of sin, they do not need to fear that God will take away His Spirit, because He has promised, *"I will never leave you and I will never abandon you" (Hebrews 13:5)*.

14. David, having received and accepted God's forgiveness, went on in his life as King of Israel. Guilt can paralyze us from serving God and make us ineffective in our pursuits. According to Hebrews 9:14, what is the result of being free from guilt?

15. ***Your life's journey:*** Are you still beating yourself up about something for which you have received forgiveness? Do you struggle with accepting the consequences and moving forward in life? What does David's acceptance of God's **complete forgiveness** teach you about forgiving yourself?

16. We are encouraged as those in Christ to be holy, which means to be set apart *from* sin and *for* God's special use (1 Peter 1:15, 2 Corinthians 7:1). As maturing Christians, we are to avoid allowing sin to reign in our bodies (Romans 6:12-14). We accomplish these admonitions by making choices. How do the following verses relate to the choices we make in our lives?

- Romans 12:1-2—

- Ephesians 4:22-32—

- Philippians 4:8-9—

Focus on the Meaning: Discipline is training that develops character, self-control or orderliness and efficiency. It is forward looking to a change of behavior and/or character, is individually tailored, personally applied, and is chiefly concerned with what will benefit the individual in question.

Though God can and does forgive our sins, He will never call sin "Okay" in order to make you feel good about yourself. The New Testament consistently declares that believers have been freed from the punishment of sins (John 3:16-18, 5:24; Romans 5:9, 8:1; 1 Thessalonians 5:9; 1 John 4:17-19). Yet, God disciplines His children in order to conform them to the likeness of His son (Romans 8:28-30; Philippians 1:6; Revelation 3:19). As believers in Christ living in the grace of God, we deal with a loving Father who teaches, trains and corrects.

17. Read Hebrews 12:7 and Proverbs 3:12. Explain how God loving us enough to discipline us is beneficial for our walk of faith towards godliness (God-likeness) for the rest of our lives.

More than 50 years after God plucked David from his father's sheepfold, God's work with David is nearly finished. We have seen a life of faith unfold as we've followed David from pasture to exile to military success as king to sinfulness and restoration.

Read 1 Chronicles 28:1-11 and 29:10-19.

18. Focus on 1 Chronicles 28:1-11. As David's life draws to a close, we read about David's parting words to the people as well as to his son, Solomon, the next king.

- Instead of reflecting on his many great accomplishments as warrior-king, on what does David focus?

Think About It: David reflects on the covenant God has made with him to bring about an enduring dynasty through David (2 Samuel 7). Rather than focusing on what he couldn't do (build the temple), he praises God for what God had given him.

- What is his advice to Solomon in the presence of all the people? See also 1 Chronicles 29:1.

19. Focus on 1 Chronicles 29:10-19, David's beautiful prayer of praise and worship. For what does he ask God?

The last words written about David's life are in 1 Chronicles 29:28a: *"He died at a good old age, having enjoyed long life, wealth, and honor ..."* What an epitaph! God was faithful to complete the good work He began in a shepherd boy many years beforehand. David faithfully served God as one of the greatest kings that ever lived and is remembered by God as "a man after my own heart."

20. ***Your life's journey:*** Though David fell in his walk of faith, he got back up and went on with his life. David was able to cling to what he knew to be true about God, such as God's sovereignty, the eternal perspective of life, and God's love for us even during times of discipline. What in David's life encourages you to persevere in a life of faith *despite* your successes or failures? Do you cling to the same truths about God that David did?

Respond to the Lord about what He's shown you today.

Recommended: *Listen to the podcast "Covered by God's Grace as You Persevere" after doing this lesson to reinforce what you have learned. Use the listener guide on the next page.*

Covered by God's Grace as You Persevere

THE HUMBLE HEART OF DAVID

- David was a man after God's own heart. He loved God. But, he was still a sinner like every human who has lived since Adam.

- When finally confronted with that sin (he knew what he had done), the greatness of David surfaces in his willingness to face his sin and to return wholeheartedly to God. His humble heart before God became a repentant heart.

- God is interested in our **heart** attitude. God responds to humble hearts willing to repent of sin and approach life God's way instead.

- Because of God's abundant grace, David was cleansed and forgiven. David could persevere in his role as king, and God could still use him as a vessel God could use for His glory.

- There is no sin that is too big for God. God knows who we are without Him—helpless, dirty rotten sinners who are enemies of God. That's why God stepped in and did something about it. *Romans 5:8*

THE AMAZING GRACE OF GOD

- What is God's grace? God's grace is His undeserved favor abundantly poured out on those who desperately need Him. God gives His grace to us because of His great love for us. *Ephesians 2:4*

- In His grace, God offers forgiveness for all our sins and gives us new life that lasts forever plus many more fabulous blessings. We receive His grace by doing one thing: putting our faith in His Son Jesus Christ. By faith alone, God's grace is given to us. And, He does that knowing we will still sin against Him. That's what is also so amazing about God's grace.

- God demonstrates His own love for us in forgiving us of those sins just because we have trusted in Jesus. By faith, we receive God's amazing grace. Not by performance or perfection. Yet, God's grace fosters an eagerness for doing good and gives us the freedom from the trap of sin.

FREEDOM FROM THE TRAP OF SIN

- Being a Christian is not equal to being a model of perfection. It is not impossible for believers to sin, but it is stupid to deliberately do so.

- When Jesus died, He released us from our bondage to sin. We have died to sin's claim on our lives. We were like prisoners who have been presented with an open door to freedom. Why would we choose to go back into the cell? Instead, we can now choose to be slaves to goodness.

- When we trusted Christ as Savior, our identity was changed. We are new spiritual creations. But, our sin nature still remains in our bodies somewhere. We still have that natural desire to go our own way. The Holy Spirit can empower us to obey God and walk in a newness of life, but He will not force us to do it. That is a choice we make each day.

- The Christian life is a process, not a one-time event. It takes perseverance every day to live by the Spirit and not walk by the flesh. You have to continually make that choice.

WALKING WITH GOD THROUGH THE CONSEQUENCES OF SIN

- Though David fell in his walk of faith, he got back up and went on with his life. He was able to cling to what he knew to be true about God, such as God's sovereignty, God's mercy, and God's love for us even during times of discipline.

- Sin cannot change our identity or position in Christ. It cannot change our eternal destiny. Those things are done deals from the moment of our salvation.

- Sin can influence how our lives look today. Sometimes we make a mess of our lives by our foolish choices and decisions. Yet, God's grace often prevents the full weight of the consequences from happening.

- When we recognize sin in our lives, we can agree with God that we have sinned (confession). Then, we can repent—turn from that sin and go God's way with our lives. Our broken heart can become a repaired heart.

- God's throne is a place of grace! Because of Jesus' shed blood on the cross, we can draw near with confidence to the throne of grace to receive mercy and find help in our time of need.

- God's grace is His undeserved favor abundantly poured out on those who desperately need him. His grace overflows to you every single day. You are completely forgiven and covered in God's grace not because you are good enough to deserve it but because His love chooses to do so. We all receive it when we trust in Jesus.

We can have hope because we have God with us. So, remember our lane markers for the race.

    #1. Choose to persevere through every challenge.
    #2. Count on God's promise to give you hope.
    #3. Let that hope sustain you through the rough-and-tumble of life.
    #4. Celebrate the joyful reward.

Let Jesus satisfy your heart with hope so you can persevere through life.

Elijah—God's Humble Prophet

8 The God of the Impossible Situation

1 Kings 17:1-18:46

For whatever was written in earlier times was written for our instruction, so that through endurance and the encouragement of the Scriptures we might have hope and overflow with confidence in His promises. (Romans 15:4, AMP)

DAY ONE STUDY

Historical Perspective

Under Saul, David and Solomon, the loosely associated 12 tribes of Israel formed one nation (1050-930 BC.). For centuries before that, though, friction had existed between the northern and southern tribes. After Solomon died (930 BC.), the 10 tribes dwelling primarily north of Jerusalem broke off and formed a new nation referred to as Israel (or, the northern kingdom) with the hilltop city of Samaria as its capital. The 2 remaining tribes—Judah and Benjamin—became known as Judah (or, the southern kingdom) with Jerusalem as its capital. For the most part, Israel's kings were idolatrous and rebellious against God. Some of Judah's kings were likewise.

Our study of Elijah begins during the reign of Ahab who became king of Israel ~70 years after the death of Solomon. Ahab married Jezebel from Sidon in Phoenicia (modern Lebanon), the birthplace of Baal worship. Jezebel was the dominant member of the marriage, and her influence had huge impact on Ahab as king and the nation as she promoted Baal worship in Israel. It had not found its way into Israel until this marriage.

Both nations, Israel and Judah, were falling deep into idol-worship, so God chose special men and women to be prophets, His mouthpieces. Some, like Elijah, were commissioned to a lifetime of service to God, while others performed one simple, yet important job. All responded to God's call to give His messages to both kings and ordinary people.

Like the books of 1 and 2 Samuel, 1 and 2 Kings originally were one book in the Hebrew Bible. The Septuagint separated them into two parts. No one knows the author of 1 and 2 Kings, which encompass a time period of more than four hundred years, but certain literary clues point to a single compiler of a number of records.

> **Recommended:** *Read or listen to 1 Kings chapters 17-22 and 2 Kings chapters 1-2 to get the "Big Picture" of Elijah's life during this study.*

1. **Deeper Discoveries (optional):** Research to find out more information about the time period in which Elijah lived.

   • What ravens eat—

   • The life of prophets—

- Baal worship and why it provoked the Lord to anger—

Read 1 Kings 17:1-24. Ask the Lord Jesus to teach you through His Word.

The mention of Elijah in 1 Kings 17:1 is abrupt. Unlike David or Joseph, we know nothing of his age, family or youth. His name combines 2 names for God: *El* (from Elohim, "God") plus *jah* (from Yahweh, the personal name God told the Hebrews to call Him). So, his name means *My God is Yahweh*. His place of birth was across the Jordan River in a land of solitude and outdoor life. The people were rugged, muscular, uneducated and unpolished. Elijah's style was likewise bold with no frills. He clothed himself in a rough, hairy garment probably woven from goat's hair and large leather belt (2 Kings 1:8). John the Baptist also wore the same distinctive apparel (Matthew 3:4).

> **Scriptural Insight:** Elijah was courageous and bold in his confrontation of Ahab with the drought pronouncement. Jezebel was killing off the Lord's prophets (1 Kings18:4).

2. Read Deuteronomy 11:13-18 and James 5:17-18. Elijah prayed according to God's promises made to Israel. We can do the same. By his own words and God's promise, Elijah knew the drought would last for several years. Let's focus first on 1 Kings 17:1-6.

- What kinds of problems accompany a drought?

- What was God's plan to care for Elijah in his *impossible situation*?

- What did Elijah learn about trusting God?

> **Think About It:** Elijah had to hide because he would be hunted by the king and queen. Hiding means a loss of independence, forcing you to trust in someone or something besides yourself. Have you recognized when God moved you away from an evil influence or danger?

3. Focus on vv. 7-16. Elijah is no longer alone dealing with an impossible situation.

- What were Elijah's life circumstances now and the choices he made?

- What were the widow's life circumstances and the choices she made?

- How was God faithful to Elijah as well as to the widow and her son?

Scriptural Insight: Whether the woman had faith in the Lord before this time doesn't matter. What does matter is that she responded in obedience to the word of the Lord, which demonstrates faith. The Lord honored her faith by fulfilling His promise miraculously. They could get this provision nowhere else. Only the true God could provide flour and oil in a drought! Only the true God can give life (next section)!

4. Focus on vv. 17-24.

   • How does Elijah deal with the difficult situation of the boy's death, a situation outside of Elijah's control? Where does he go? How does he react?

   • How did Elijah's knowledge of and faith in God benefit this family?

   Focus on the Meaning: When the boy died, the woman immediately entertained error in her thinking, "God is punishing me for my sin by killing my son. It's all my fault." This is a common reaction among many people who do not know God or His ways when personal tragedy enters their lives. But, it is wrong thinking. Although some hardship comes as the consequence of a person's wrong choices (as in David's later life), most does not as we have seen in our study so far. Based on our study of Joseph, was he put into slavery or jailed as a consequence of his behavior? No! Was David on the run from Saul for 13 years because of his own fault? No! And, God was with both of them.

5. Read the following verses to see what God says regarding this error in our thinking:

   • John 9:1-3—

   • Matthew 7:24-27—

   • Romans 8:1—

6. *Your life's journey:* We will focus on a 3-part application to this lesson, all centered on what to do with an *impossible situation*.

   • **Step #1: Identify it.** What are you (or someone close to you) facing today that is bleak and/or impossible?

- **Step #2: Think rightly about it.** What's your usual response when tragedy strikes or when a test comes? Based upon what we have learned so far in this study, is this the correct (Biblical) response? Are you blaming yourself (or someone else), thinking that God is punishing you with this impossible situation? If you are, go back and review the verses you read in Question 5.

- **Step #3: Bring it to God.** *Trust that God loves you, He knows what is going on in your life, and He can do something about it.* Read Psalm 27:14; Luke 1:37; and Matthew 19:25-26 for encouragement as you deal with your impossible situation. Place on your "bed" that critical situation—that burden that is burning your energy, weighing on your mind. Review how God has gotten you through an impossible situation in the past. **God is still the God of impossible situations today!**

Think About It: Reflect on one man's choice of how to think in a difficult time: First, God brought me here. It is by His will that I am in this straight place. In that fact, I will rest. Next, God will keep me here in His love, and *He will give me grace to behave as His child.* Then, God will make the trial a blessing, teaching me the lessons He intends me to learn and working in me the grace He means to bestow. Last, in God's good time, He can bring me out again—how and when, He knows. Let me say, I am here: 1) by God's appointment, 2) in His keeping, 3) under His training, 4) for His time. Amen. (*In Quietness and Confidence,* Dr. Raymond Edmund)

Respond to the Lord about what He's shown you today.

Day Two Study

The Showdown

Baal was the Canaanites' chief fertility god as well as the storm god in charge of clouds, wind, and rain—all necessary for crops to grow. Ancient statues show him gripping a lightning bolt in his left hand, ready to hurl it as a spear toward earth. As such, Baal was a God substitute. The three-and-one-half year drought had been a great embarrassment to worshipers of Baal. So, Elijah's test to Baal's followers seemed like a good opportunity to vindicate their "god" and they readily agreed to it.

This chapter (1 Kings 18) is one of the most significant chapters of the Bible. It could be titled "Winner Takes All" or "The Fight of the Century." It is the showdown between the living God of heaven and the idols of men on earth.

Read 1 Kings 18:1-19. Ask the Lord Jesus to teach you through His Word.

7. Elijah was a wanted man; Ahab thought of him as a snake, a viper. No doubt, the stench of death was all around. The famine was severe by now.

- What was Elijah commanded to do and how did he respond (vv. 1, 18-19)?

- Besides Elijah, who else was learning about faith in God at this time? How?

Read I Kings 18:20-40.

Desperate for an end to the drought, Ahab agrees to Elijah's demands. Probably hundreds, if not thousands of people, gathered since Elijah summoned all Israel to Mount Carmel (1500 feet above sea level). There are 3 main groups represented at this showdown: the "No Comment Fence-Sitter" Israelites, Ahab plus Jezebel's Baalites, and Elijah plus God. Let's look at them one at a time to glean our lessons.

> **Historical Insight:** Elijah chose this mountain, as God led him, because it stood between Israel and Phoenicia geographically, neutral ground between Yahweh's land and Baal's. Furthermore, the Phoenicians regarded Carmel as a sacred dwelling place of Baal. Storms with lightning and thunder were common on Mount Carmel, and Baal worshippers viewed them as manifestations of their deity. The name "Carmel" means "the garden land," and it was famous for its fertility. In the minds of many, Baal had the advantage in this contest. (*Dr. Constable's Notes on 1 Kings 2014 Edition*, p. 70)

8. **The "No Comment Fence-Sitters" of Israel:**

- Why was this showdown necessary for them (vv. 21-22)?

- What condition did he set up to prove the truth (v. 24)?

- What did Elijah do in vv. 31-32, 36 to remind them of their identity?

> **Think About It:** There is only one way to determine your identity that cannot be shaken, one foundation that cannot be taken away from you: "I am a child of God." Now you might be a child of God who happens to be a businessman...or a mother...or an athlete. But the core source of your identity is your relationship with your God and Father. Only in this way can you ever begin to discover true security...At moments of

failure, we need to be reminded of who we really are so that we can return to dependency upon Him and act in accordance with our true identity. We never outgrow our need to be reminded of who we are in Christ! It is something that God is trying to teach us from the first day of our Christian lives until the day we go home to heaven, and this truth provides a constant standard against which we learn to measure our thinking and responses throughout life. (Bob George, *Growing in Grace*, p. 22, 63)

Divided allegiance is as wrong as open idolatry. It is likely that hundreds, if not thousands, congregated on Mount Carmel in answer to Elijah's directive for Ahab to summon them (v. 19). The people were lukewarm toward God, "straddling the fence," perhaps trying to combine both religions. The easiest thing to do in the hour of decision is to remain uncommitted. But, with God, it's either/or, not both. Our God wants our hearts to be completely His!

9. Read James 4:4 and Revelation 3:15-16. What does the Bible say about people who try to "straddle the fence?"

Think About It: When we stray away from Christ as our life, we have no alternative but to return to self-generated, self-centered, and self-disciplined religious experience and the "counsel of the ungodly." (Bob George, *Growing in Grace*, p. 36)

10. **Ahab + Jezebel's Baalites:** Elijah had Baal's prophets set up an altar and a sacrifice but with instructions to pray to their god to light the wood for them. Elijah did the same. The one who answered by fire would be the true God.

   *   What things did Baal's prophets do for 6 hours to get their god's attention to light the fire?

Scriptural Insight: Such mutilation of the body was strictly forbidden in the Mosaic law (Leviticus 19:28; Deuteronomy 14:1). (*NIV Study Bible 1985 Edition*, note on 1 Kings 18:27, p. 511)

   *   In what ways did Elijah mock Baal, thus refusing to acknowledge that he was a god at all?

   *   How did Baal answer?

11. **Elijah plus God:**

- What had Elijah learned about God over the previous 3 years that prepared him for this very public challenge?

- How did Elijah set up the challenge to make it an even more impossible situation?

- How did Elijah approach God to answer the challenge (vv. 36-37)?

- How did God answer?

- How did the people respond?

   Focus on the Meaning: At the time of the Israelites' evening sacrifice, Elijah stepped forward and prayed. Without any of the theatrics of his adversaries, Elijah simply addressed God as one addresses anther living person. His words demonstrated to the onlookers that all he had done as God's servant had been in obedience to God's command and not on his own initiative. (*The Bible Knowledge Commentary Old Testament*, p. 527)

12. ***Your life's journey:*** God's purpose for this showdown was to "turn the hearts back again to Himself." Follow the steps below to overcome being a "no comment fence-sitter" in your life.

- **Step 1: Choose to become committed to God and His ways.** One of God's purposes was to turn the hearts of the people back to Himself. This involves a choice. If you haven't made this choice for your life already, why not do it today?

- **Step 2: Choose to stay committed.** *Read the following questions and answer any that apply to your life.* Have you felt that tension between your Christian faith (often snubbed as "traditional") and the pull of your modern culture? In what ways is the tension most challenging to you and why? Have you sometimes been tempted to desert some of God's ways to fit in better by taking the "embrace the best of both worlds" approach? Or, have you stood firm for God and His ways in spite of opposition? What have been the results of any of these choices?

Respond to the Lord about what He's shown you today.

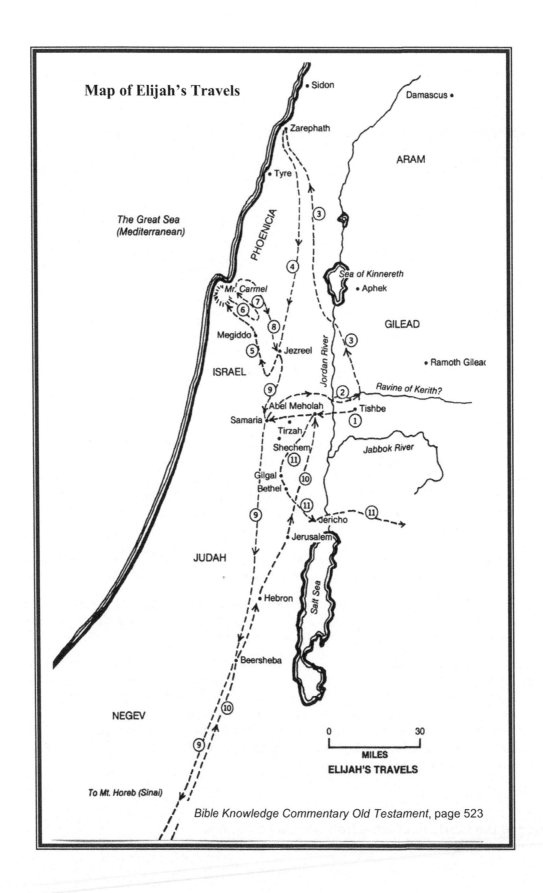

Map of Elijah's Travels

Bible Knowledge Commentary Old Testament, page 523

DAY THREE STUDY

Read 1 Kings 18:41-46. Ask the Lord Jesus to teach you through His Word.

13. Let's look at how God, through Elijah, finished up His Mount Carmel demonstration. Elijah's words to the stunned and spiritually defeated Ahab showed Elijah's unwavering trust in God.

- Describe Elijah's persistence to see God's promise in 18:1 fulfilled (vv. 41-45).

- How did God show His power (vv. 45-46)?

- What did Elijah, his servant, and Ahab learn about God that day?

In 1 Kings 18:15, Elijah refers to God as "The Lord Almighty (NIV)." This title for God reflects the fact that God has all the forces of heaven at His disposal to accomplish His will, that He is more powerful than any earthy army or kingdom and any cosmic force, and that He strikes down His people's adversaries and delivers His own. On Mount Carmel, Yahweh demonstrated that He is truly "The Lord Almighty."

14. *Your life's journey:* In what ways does your life reflect the reality of God's being Lord Almighty? For instance, do you find reassurance in His power or have you experienced His help? Are there some fearful situations that you have given over to Him?

Think About It: Our day is characterized by mediocrity. Christians blend into the scenery of the times. God looks for special people at such difficult times, and His methods are often surprising. We expect flash; He uses ordinary, everyday lives. He uses women who are engaged in constant ministry to their families in their homes. It may be to only 1, 2, or 3 people. We shouldn't look down on that. What we must remember is that first and foremost, we stand before God. He looks for men and women whose hearts are completely His, who won't blend into the scenery of their culture, bowing the knee to idols. God found a man who was completely His. Would God find you to be completely His today?

15. *Your life's journey:* As Elijah did, you can make the choice to be committed to God and the specific job He has given you to do. Elijah points out the truth and doesn't back down. John Knox, Scottish evangelist of the 1600s, once said, "God and one are a majority." Never

underestimate the influence of one unique, totally dedicated life. Allow God to grow you so that you can become the Elijah in your sphere of influence.

Consider 2 people in your sphere of influence who need to know the one true God and commit to pray for God to reveal Himself to them in an unmistakable manner. In confidence, step into their lives demonstrating God's love for them while you wait for God to work.

Respond to the Lord about what He's shown you today.

Recommended: *Listen to the podcast "The God You Can Know" after doing this lesson to reinforce what you have learned. Use the listener guide on the next page.*

The God You Can Know

Like other prophets in the Bible, Elijah knew who God was and understood His character. Prophets didn't just predict future events. They more often taught people in the present about the God they served or claimed to serve. Prophets taught theology.

WHAT IS THEOLOGY?

- Theology is simply what you believe about God. Whether we want to call ourselves that or not, we are the theologians in our spheres of influence. And, it matters if we are good ones or not. It matters what we know about God and relate about Him by words or actions to those around us.

  Your life is your billboard. And every day, you can choose the message to display.
  (Jayme Durant, *Acts & Facts*, 48 (11), p. 4)

- Understanding the truth about God and being able to communicate that truth in casual conversation and serious discussion is one of your greatest assets for any relationship. You use your theology to give others strength or drag them down.

- We learn theology like we learn most anything else in life: Prepare by instruction, learn by experience. Prepare by instruction means studying the truths about God in the Bible. Learn by experience means to trust in what you believe about God as you live out your life. We can face any impossible situation if we are prepared by instruction about God and teachable to learn through experience with God.

THE GOD YOU CAN KNOW

God demonstrated things about Himself to Elijah and through Elijah that teach us truths about Him today.

1. **The true God is ALIVE.** Four times Elijah refers to God as the one who lives. He is the living, active, ever-present Lord.

2. **The true God is FAITHFUL.** Our God is a promise-keeping God. God promised to feed Elijah and the widow and to send rain. God kept those promises.

3. **The true God is EVERYWHERE at once.** While God was present in Jerusalem in the Temple at this time, He was also present with Elijah and with the widow in Phoenicia. And, He never sleeps.

4. **The true God is LOVING.** God showed Himself to these people of Israel even though they were not worshipping Him. They were rebelling against Him. That's His love.

5. **The true God is HOLY and JUST.** The people of Israel repented and declared the Lord to be God. The prophets of Baal did not repent so they were judged and removed.

6. **The true God is POWERFUL and VICTORIOUS.** When God takes charge to prove to humans that He is who He says He is, there is no interference. Satan was shut down from operating.

7. **The true God is MERCIFUL and GRACIOUS.** He promised rain before the people had even repented. He sent rain although Ahab never repented. He allowed Ahab to live. He demonstrated Himself to Ahab in an unmistakable fashion yet Ahab still rejected Him.

KNOWING THE TRUTH ABOUT GOD LEADS TO CHOICES

What was the single most important event in human history? The cross followed by the resurrection. A gigantic Z. God demonstrated His **power** over our greatest enemy, sin and its consequence—death. God demonstrated His **love** in that He did this while we were still His enemies. God demonstrated His **justice** in a sinless Jesus who became sin for us and took that penalty for sin that we deserved—death. God demonstrated His **grace** in that He offered this payment for our sin so that we might be declared righteous, perfectly acceptable to Him, by faith. Our responsibility is to accept His plan. There is only one way to the true God—by faith in His Son Jesus Christ. That's His plan.

Our first choice is to commit ourselves to Him.

That's the same choice Elijah gave to the No Comment Fence-Sitter Israelites. It's either being for God or not for Him. You are on one side or the other. Being on the fence is on the other side. Trusting in Jesus Christ is committing ourselves to God.

Our second choice is to serve Him no matter what.

Serving God no matter what requires taking your stand before God and acting by faith in His name.

- To take one's stand means "to present oneself, to hold one's ground, and to station oneself." Picture Elijah being physically in the presence of King Ahab as he issued the drought declaration. But, in his mind and heart, he was standing in front of God. Take your stand.

- To act by faith in His name means to obey God. When the Lord told Elijah to go and confront Ahab and the Israelites, Elijah chose to go. He was given a task to confront his culture, and he did it. He acted in obedience to God's commands and not done on his own initiative. He set up the scene so that God would get the glory.

- To act by faith also means to pray and trust God to work. Elijah called upon the Lord Almighty. The God of unlimited power. Our God is exalted above the heavens. We can pray to Him, having total confidence that He loves us, He knows what is going on, and He can do something about it. Leaving it in His hands is our choice. What He does is His.

Women need good theology so we don't get caught sitting on the fence like the Israelites did. So, we won't do harm when family and friends depend on us for counsel. We need good theology to teach others rightly about God, giving them the best information to make their own decision about the God we know and serve. The God who answered by fire in Elijah's day never tires of hearing us individually stand before Him and say, "The LORD, He is MY God." He is the God you can know and trust.

We can have hope because we have God with us. So, remember our lane markers for the race.

- #1. Choose to persevere through every challenge.
- #2. Count on God's promise to give you hope.
- #3. Let that hope sustain you through the rough-and-tumble of life.
- #4. Celebrate the joyful reward.

Let Jesus satisfy your heart with hope so you can persevere through life.

Elijah—God's Humble Prophet

9 The God Who Loves You as You Are

1 Kings 19–2 Kings 2

For whatever was written in earlier times was written for our instruction, so that through perseverance and the encouragement of the Scriptures we might have hope. (Romans 15:4, NASB)

DAY ONE STUDY

1. ***Deeper Discoveries (optional):*** Research to find out more information about the time period in which Elijah lived.

   - Mount Horeb—

   - The mantle worn by Elijah—

   - The horses and chariots of fire—

After the phenomenal experience on Mt. Carmel, you might expect to find Elijah openly preaching to all Israel. Instead…

Read 1 Kings 19:1-18. Ask the Lord Jesus to teach you through His Word.

2. Jezebel sent a message to Elijah that basically said, "You are a dead man."

   - What is Elijah's first response?

   - Where is he heading? (See the map in the first Elijah lesson to follow Elijah's travels.)

   - What thoughts about his situation does he vocalize to God in prayer (v. 4)?

   - Considering the great victory on Mt. Carmel, when Elijah stood alone but boldly proclaimed God, what could be the reasons he now lost courage?

3. What help does God send to Elijah for his dejected condition and his journey?

> **Think About It:** In 1 Kings 19:9, the Hebrew text says, "He came to **the** cave," possibly the very cleft of the rock where God had placed Moses as His glory passed by (Ex. 33:14-23). The Lord told Moses, "My presence shall go with you, and I will give you rest." What might Elijah have been seeking at Mt. Horeb?

4. Arriving at the cave on Mt. Horeb, Elijah sleeps. When he awakes,

    •   What question does the Lord ask Elijah twice?

    •   What answer does Elijah give to the Lord twice?

    •   What does God do in vv. 11-12?

    •   How does Elijah respond to the gentle whisper (v 13)?

5. What are God's words of encouragement and instruction to Elijah?

Our God understands our weaknesses, failures, and needs. Fear, confusion and despair distorted Elijah's thinking, and he ran first before praying. He withdrew from his sphere of influence and neglected his body's needs. He wallowed in self-pity. He became weak because He stopped trusting God. God responded to Elijah's need. Did you notice all the specific ways God helped, encouraged, and showed His love for Elijah? Although God can and does display His power in mighty acts like that on Mt. Carmel (1 Kings 18), the majority of us experience His presence as Elijah did—the gentle "whisper." Personal. For us alone. As Christians, God "draws" us to Himself in a loving personal relationship. We have access to His "power" daily. You can say to yourself, "God loves me as I am." How can we NOT be drawn to a God who loves us in this way?

6. ***Your life's journey:***

- Have you ever followed Elijah's stressed-out steps? What happened, and how did God help you out of such a painful place in the past?

- Read John 14:16-17 and Romans 8:26-27. How has God already provided for us the way to know His presence and power?

- Read Hebrews 4:14-16; Psalm 56:3-4; and 1 Peter 5:7. What does He tell us to do with our fears?

Scriptural Insight: Preventing despair is far easier than recovery! Next time you encounter a frightening situation, dwell on the verses you just read.

Respond to the Lord about what He's shown you today.

DAY TWO STUDY

Read 1 Kings 19:15-21. Ask the Lord Jesus to teach you through His Word.

A Partner in Ministry

7. In response to God's instructions, what did Elijah do?

8. Like Elijah, Elisha was a nobody. In what ways might Elisha have encouraged Elijah during his years of service to the prophet?

Think About It: God can achieve His purpose either through the absence of human power and resources or the abandonment of reliance upon them. All through history God has chosen and used nobodies, because their unusual dependence on Him made possible the unique display of his power and grace. He chose and used "somebodies" only when they renounced dependence on their natural abilities and resources. (Oswald Chambers)

Elisha's first ministry was simply to become Elijah's friend. To be a listening ear, to offer words of counsel. To just be there. It was true that Elisha poured water over Elijah's hands as a servant. But more important than that, he poured the refreshing water of encouragement over Elijah's heart as a close companion. For ten years, until the older prophet was finally called into the presence of the Lord, Elisha served Elijah, walked the dusty roads of Samaria with him, and stood by his side until the very end.

9. *Your life's journey:* It's easy to overlook a ministry of friendship and encouragement. Often it goes unnoticed. It isn't the kind of ministry that grabs a lot of attention and headlines. Jonathan was David's friend at a critical time in David's life. David went on to the throne and to fame and renown, but it was Jonathan who had stood beside him. It was Jonathan who had encouraged the son of Jesse when David felt like life wasn't worth living. Paul initiated the major first-century thrust for Christian missions, but as you read his letters you discover it was several supportive friends who made the difference in his life, especially Barnabas and Silas.

Has God called you to a "background" ministry of encouragement? How?

Think it through: Your infinitely creative God delights in diversity! That's why He created you exactly the way you are. He has gifted you with the ability to reflect the life of Jesus Christ in a way that no one else who ever walked the earth (or ever will) can hope to duplicate. Have you found the freedom to be yourself in your ministry and not have to match someone else's style, results or expectations? (Adapted from *Talk through the Bible,* Dr. Bruce Wilkinson, pages 116-123)

The Bold Elijah Once Again

Ahab had his eye on a piece of land next to his summer palace. He wanted it bad, bad. But, the owner Naboth would not sell because it was his family's ancestral land. Ahab got angry and sullen. Jezebel spread rumors about Naboth making him a target to get stoned. End of Naboth. Jezebel proudly told her husband to go and take the land. But, God was watching all this unfold, and He wasn't finished using Elijah as his messenger of judgment to Ahab.

Read 1 Kings 21:17-29.

10. Describe the interaction between Ahab and Elijah this time (vv. 21-26).

11. What resulted (vv. 27-29)?

In chapter 22, we see how the Lord was true to His word. Ahab died in battle. Then, it was Jezebel's turn. Several court officials who were tired of her brutality exacted God's vengeance on her. Next comes God's judgment on Ahab's son.

Read 2 Kings 1:1-18.

12. Ahaziah was as wicked as his mother and father. He consulted a fortune teller (representing the occult) to find out if he would recover from an injury.

   - How did God continue to use Elijah (vv. 3-4)?

   - Elijah departed to do what God sent him to do. Ahaziah sent soldiers to intercept and kill him. When the captain ordered the one representing God to come with him, what was God's response through Elijah (vv.9-12)?

   - When the third captain showed respect for God and God's representative, how did Elijah respond this time (vv. 13-18)?

13. *Your life's journey:* Many people—Christians included—get involved in harmless activities, thinking that they're fun and harmless things to do. But, harmless and powerless they are not. To remain unaware of the truth is to leave yourself naively unprotected against Satan's schemes.

   - Have you dabbled in the occult? Reading your horoscope just for kicks. Visiting the fortune teller at the county fair? Bringing out the Ouija board or tarot cards to spice up a party? If so, has your involvement affected you or others? How?

   - Did you realize you were turning away from God when doing so? Do you know how offended the Lord is by this?

- Ask the Lord to release you (and/or your family members) from any occult entanglements that still have you bound. Find verses to use in prayer such as Colossians 1:13-14.

Respond to the Lord about what He's shown you today.

DAY THREE STUDY

A No-Death Contract

As a prophet, Elijah represented God during the time period 875-848 BC. That means for 27 years, he remained faithful and persevered through drought and discouragement. This perseverance produced fruit in his own life, as well as in the life of Elisha whom he trained to take over after him. He most likely also spent time at the various schools of the prophets, also called the "sons of the prophets" or "company of the prophets," located at Gilgal, Bethel, and Jericho where men were in training for the life of a prophet—the earliest "seminaries." These schools were apparently begun by Samuel to teach the Israelites the revealed Word of God and encouraged by Elijah as he visited them. What an abundant life Elijah led!!

Read 2 Kings 2:1-18. Ask the Lord Jesus to teach you through His Word.

14. Discuss the interaction between Elijah and Elisha (vv. 1-6).

15. After crossing the Jordan River, what did Elisha request? How did Elijah answer?

16. Describe what happened next (vv. 11-14).

Think About It: It was not Elisha's mannerisms, style, or methods he had requested; it was Elijah's strength and spirit. Now, endowed with the strength, Elisha was free to utilize his own gifts—he was free to be himself. If you were Elisha, gifted with a double portion of Elijah's spirit and launched into your own career as a prophet, how would you begin to shape your ministry?

17. What did those 50 men from the "company of the prophets" witness?

Scriptural Insight: Elisha was one of those persons who lived much of his life in the shadow of a great individual. Elijah was the prophet of fire. Elisha's ministry was less dramatic. Even after Elijah was gone from the scene and Elisha was well-established in his own work, he was still known as the man who "used to pour water on the hands of Elijah" (2 Kings 3:11). For generations, a special chair has been set for Elijah at the circumcision ceremonies of every Jewish boy. Even though the Bible records twice as many miracles of God through Elisha as He did through Elijah, the former would probably be content to be remembered as the man who followed Elijah.

18. ***Your life's journey:*** One day, many Christians will also be taken up directly to heaven without seeing death. Read 1 Thessalonians 4:13-18. This is commonly called the Rapture, a much-anticipated event for it signals the time when Christ will come to defeat His enemies on earth and set up His earthly kingdom. Thinking about Elijah, what would you do if you knew today was your last day on earth?

Scriptural Insight: The influence of Elijah did not end here nor was God finished using Him to do His will. In Malachi 4:5-6, God promises "behold, I will send you Elijah the prophet before the coming of the great and dreadful day of the Lord. And he shall turn the heart of the fathers to the children, and the heart of the children to their fathers, lest I come and smite the earth with a curse." This expectation of the return of Elijah appears frequently in the New Testament. In the gospels, the Jews thought both John the Baptist and Jesus were Elijah. Along with Moses, Elijah did appear to Jesus on the Mount of Transfiguration (see Mark 9:4-5). When Jesus was not welcomed into a Samaritan village, James and John wanted to call down fire from heaven as Elijah did. Some thought Jesus called for Elijah to rescue Him from the cross. In the book of James, Elijah is used an example of an ordinary man who persisted in prayer. Whether Elijah is one of the two witnesses, together with Enoch, in Revelation 11, is a matter of interpretation, resting on the fact that Enoch and Elijah are the only two men recorded as being taken up to heaven without dying.

19. ***Your life's journey:*** What in Elijah's life encourages you to persevere?

Respond to the Lord about what He's shown you today.

> **Recommended:** *Listen to the podcast "How Deep Our Father's Love for Us" after doing this lesson to reinforce what you have learned. Use the listener guide on the next page.*

How Deep Our Father's Love for Us

HOW DEEP OUR FATHER GOD'S LOVE

You cannot look at 1 Kings chapter 19 without realizing how much God loved Elijah. Elijah is running away, exhausted, afraid, and disappointed. He didn't ask God about it first. He just reacted to the threat on his life and ran. Elijah's target was Mt. Sinai, the place where God made the initial covenant with Israel accompanied by fire and smoke and thunder. Yet, God intercepted him on the way, sent an angel to feed him, and whispered to him outside that cave. God gave him encouragement, a friend, and tasks to do. That deep, fatherly love bolstered Elijah to persevere as God's prophet for several more years.

> *I am always with you; you hold me by my right hand. You guide me with your counsel, and afterward you will take me into glory. Whom have I in heaven but you? And earth has nothing I desire besides you. My flesh and my heart may fail, but God is the strength of my heart and my portion forever. (Psalm 73:23-26)*

GOD HOLDS ME BY MY RIGHT HAND

> *"My grace is enough for you, for my power is made perfect in weakness." (2 Corinthians 12:9)*

- Picture yourself sitting in Jesus' lap, holding out your hand for Father God to take hold and whisper in your ear, "Don't be afraid, I am helping you."

- Our God is a trustworthy Father. Jesus continually taught His disciples to consider God as their Father. This God is your Father God, too. The moment you placed your trust in Jesus Christ for your salvation, you were adopted into God's family as His child. He is the perfect Father, the most loving Father, the most dependable Father, and the Father who cares about your every need. Our Father God's love for you is deep and amazing.

> *"See what amazing love the Father has given us! Because of it, we are called children of God. And that's what we really are!" (1 John 3:1)*

- Jesus continually encouraged His followers to call God, "Father." He taught them to pray to their Father God, whom they could trust.

- If you didn't have such a good earthly father, He wants you to know that you are dearly loved by your Father God. Dearly loved. Think of the best father in any book, movie, or TV show. Who comes to mind? God is even better than that father. And, you can know Him well, love Him wholeheartedly, and gain the confidence to trust Him as your Father God who loves you.

GOD GUIDES ME WITH HIS COUNSEL

- God guided Elijah with His counsel and Elijah followed it.

- The Bible guides us with God's counsel. We should desire God's counsel so we can approach life His way rather than our own.

GOD WILL TAKE ME INTO GLORY

- God certainly took Elijah into glory in a dramatic way. Fiery chariots accompanying the whirlwind that lifted him upward to heaven. An unforgettable scene for Elisha and the 50 men watching it.

- God will hold your hand all the way through this life and past this life into the glorious next one. You have a future with God in heaven. One day, Jesus will come for you.

GOD IS MY STRENGTH AND MY PORTION

- God is your strength. You can choose God every day that you are on this earth. Your flesh and heart may fail, but God is your strength now and will continue to be your strength.

- God is your portion. When a biblical writer says, "God is my portion," he means that God is the source of his happiness and blessing. He is content with all that the Lord is and provides. He has the best inheritance imaginable and does not seek any possession or comfort outside of God.

- You can persevere through anything in this life if we believe that when we have God, we need nothing else. And, our God is the one who loves us dearly with a deep Father's love.

We can have hope because we have God with us. So, remember our lane markers for the race.

- #1. Choose to persevere through every challenge.
- #2. Count on God's promise to give you hope.
- #3. Let that hope sustain you through the rough-and-tumble of life.
- #4. Celebrate the joyful reward.

Let Jesus satisfy your heart with hope so you can persevere through life.

Nehemiah—God's Servant Leader

10 A Leader Who Prayed and Worked While Praying
Nehemiah 1 – 6

Everything written in the past was written to teach us. The Scriptures give us strength to go on. They encourage us and give us hope. (Romans 15:4, NIRV)

DAY ONE STUDY

Historical Perspective

God had promised Israel that if they obeyed Him, He would bless them as a nation. If they did not, then He would judge them and cause them to be taken into captivity (Deuteronomy 28). As God had forewarned, His hand of judgment fell on all of Israel because of their sin. The Northern Kingdom (Israel) fell first and the people were taken into captivity by the Assyrians in 722 BC. The Babylonians brought about the fall of the Southern Kingdom (Judah) in 586 BC.

The Israelites of the Northern Kingdom were absorbed into Assyria and eventually into other cultures. However, the people of the Southern kingdom remained intact in Babylon, and after the power of Babylon was broken by the Medes and the Persians in 539 BC., many Jews returned to their homeland. In 538 BC. the first group returned to Judah under the leadership of Zerubbabel (Ezra 1:1-2:2).

Over a period of years and tremendous opposition from the Samaritans, the returnees eventually succeeded in rebuilding the temple in 515 BC. Ezra, the priest, then led another return to Israel and restored worship in the rebuilt temple in Jerusalem. Nehemiah also returned in 444 BC., 14 years after Ezra's return to Jerusalem, and God used him to guide Judah in rebuilding the city's walls and in reordering the people's social and economic lives. What he accomplished in a brief period of time was an incredible feat. How he stayed dependent on God and stayed focused on his task to accomplish this goal is one of the major emphases in the book that bears his name.

The book of Nehemiah is a personal account written by Nehemiah himself. No information is given about Nehemiah's childhood, his adolescent years, or even about his family, with the exception of his father's name (Hacaliah) and one brother (Hanani).

> **Recommended:** *Read or listen to Ezra, Esther, & Nehemiah to get the "Big Picture" of Nehemiah's life during this study.*

1. **Deeper Discoveries (optional):** Research to find more information about the time period in which Nehemiah lived.

   • Scrolls and writing—

   • The significance of city walls and gates—

   • Sackcloth—

Historical Insight: "...It was the cupbearer's responsibility to taste the king's wine before it was served to make sure that no one had poisoned it. In those days of totalitarian monarchs, assassination was the only way one could be removed from office. The usual method was to poison his food or his wine. This was a dangerous job Nehemiah had. It is obvious that he had to be a man of unlimited integrity and trustworthiness. The king relied upon him to keep him safe. He must always be above suspicion, keeping the king's trust at all times. If the king grew suspicious or distrustful, Nehemiah's life would be in danger. He would not only lose his job; he could also lose his head." (Ray Stedman, Sermon notes, January 8, 1989)

Read Nehemiah 1:1-11. Ask the Lord Jesus to teach you through His Word.

As the book of Nehemiah begins, Nehemiah is employed as cupbearer to the King of Persia, King Artaxerxes. As you read the book of Nehemiah, notice its personal, eyewitness perspective.

2. Nehemiah got some not-so-good news. See also Ezra 4:18-23 for additional insight.

   • What was the news?

   • How did Nehemiah respond to the news he was given?

   • What does Nehemiah's response reveal about his character?

3. Focusing on Nehemiah's prayer in vv. 5-11.

   • What do you learn about his understanding of God's justice?

   • What do you learn about his understanding of God's love?

   • What was his request of God?

   Scriptural Insight: Nehemiah speaks of God as the "great and awesome God" in 1:5; 4:14; and 9:32. That was his view of God and how he portrayed God to the Jewish people.

Read Nehemiah 2:1-9.

Nehemiah received the report about Jerusalem and began praying in the month of Kislev (November-December) and now it is Nisan (March-April), four months of praying later.

4. What do you observe Nehemiah choosing to say and do in this time of opportunity before the King?

5. How did God answer Nehemiah's prayer from 1:11-12?

Scriptural Insight: Nehemiah's prayer and action is an illustration of the two aspects of trusting God. 1) You must trust Him as you step forward and do your part His way. 2) You must trust God to do His part in the areas over which you have no control. Those two aspects of trusting God are necessary to act on whatever God has placed in your heart to do or for any situation where you find yourself threatened.

Read Nehemiah 2:11-20.

The king gave Nehemiah supplies and authority as Judah's designated governor (5:14). That's why he got the armed escort on the trip to Jerusalem.

6. After arriving in Jerusalem, discuss the wise actions that Nehemiah took at first (vv. 11-16).

7. Then, what did he do next to get the people onboard with the project (vv. 17-19)?

8. As for most good things, there is usually opposition. From vv. 10 and 19-20, what was the opposition, and how did Nehemiah respond?

Historical Insight: These three officials show up frequently in Nehemiah so it helps to know who they are. Sanballat was the governor of Samaria (that region north and west of Jerusalem that comprised the northern kingdom of Israel). Tobiah was the governor of the region called Transjordan. He had a close relationship with Eliashib the High Priest which gave him access to what was going on within Jerusalem. Geshem was governor of northern Arabia. The opposition of all three seemed to be more political jealousy rather than anything religious. (*NIV Study Bible 1985 Edition,* notes on Nehemiah 2:10 and 2:19, pp. 695-696)

9. *Your life's journey:* Nehemiah, in his prayer and his actions, focused on God's power and glory more than on the situation alone. Think of one or two areas in your life that most concern you at this time.

   - When you pray for these situations or people, do you tend to focus more upon God and His power or upon the situation?

   - How do you think focusing more upon God and who He is might affect your ability to persevere through these times?

Respond to the Lord about what He's shown you today.

DAY TWO STUDY

Ask the Lord Jesus to teach you through His Word.

Nehemiah faced many difficult issues as he pressed on and led God's people through the task of rebuilding the wall. But the importance of the task was indisputable. The wall of an ancient city symbolized strength and protection. The building of the walls would fill the need for security and strength among the inhabitants. For instance, the walls of the city of Babylon as recounted in the story of Daniel were 380 feet thick and over 100 feet high, therefore the city of Babylon was considered very safe! The ruins of the wall around Jerusalem had been there for over 100 years and approximately 1.5 miles of the wall needed to be rebuilt to a thickness of 9 feet.

10. Nehemiah chapter 3 gives information about those who participated in rebuilding the walls. This is communal participation. Scan the chapter. Who worked? Who didn't? Where did many of them work? What else grabbed your attention?

Scriptural Insight: All priests had to be from the tribe of Levi (Levites) and specifically descendants of Aaron according to the Law. The top-ranking priest was called the "High Priest" and was the only one who could enter the "Holy of Holies"—innermost room of the Temple where God's presence dwelled. Those from the tribe of Levi who did not descend from Aaron had other duties to perform and were collectively called "the Levites" to distinguish them from the priests. The Levites were supposed to serve as teachers and administrators of God's Law in their home districts. During their turn to serve God at the Temple, they supported the worship of God's people meeting together. In that way, they were similar to pastors and church staff in today's local congregations.

Read Nehemiah 4:1-22.

The opposition continued as they worked on the walls as described in chapter 3. Nehemiah needed to lead the people through all the challenges they faced. We will look at the problems/challenges brought to Nehemiah's attention and then how he responded to them.

11. Focus on vv. 1-6.

- What is the problem / challenge?

- How do Nehemiah and the Jewish people respond?

12. Focus on vv. 7-9.

- What is the problem / challenge?

- How do Nehemiah and the Jewish people respond?

13. Focus on vv. 10-15.

- What is the problem / challenge?

- How do Nehemiah and the Jewish people respond?

Think About It: Discontent goes viral when we focus on the things we cannot control instead of the One who controls it all. (Kris Murphy, *God Reveals We Respond*, p. 10-3)

14. Focus on vv. 16-23. Discuss what they decided to do to stand firm and keep moving forward on their wall-rebuilding project.

15. ***Your life's journey:*** Looking back over today's questions,

- Why doesn't God stop the opposition? What good did it do for them? What good does it do for us?

- What are some of the lessons you learn from the responses of Nehemiah and the people? How do these lessons both encourage and teach you positive ways to deal with challenges and problems in your own life so that God is honored? Think of your home, your workplace or any other positions of leadership you have.

Respond to the Lord about what He's shown you today.

Day Three Study

Read Nehemiah 5:1-19. Ask the Lord Jesus to teach you through His Word.

Problems and challenges are not only those that come in the way of opposition from outsiders. As you saw in chapter 4, alarmists within a community can cause widespread panic. Nehemiah recognized another threat to the Jewish community that was fueled by greed.

16. Focus on vv. 1-13.

- What problem surfaced?

- Discuss what Nehemiah said and did in response to this news.

- How did the people respond?

17. Focus on vv. 14-19. What do you learn about Nehemiah as God's servant leader? Give verses to support your answer.

Think About It: One of the most helpful things that we can do to resist temptation {or distractions} is to remember that God has called us to a great task. This is true of every believer in Christ. I do not care how young or old you are in the Lord, you are called to a tremendous work today. That task is: to model a different lifestyle so that those who are being ruined by wrongful practices will see something that offers them hope and deliverance. If they see in you peace in the midst of confusion, an invisible support that keeps you steady and firm under pressure, they will learn that there is another way to live than the destructive ways they have chosen. That is the great work that God has called us to. We ought never to give allegiance to anything less. (Ray Stedman, Sermon notes, January 29, 1989)

Read Nehemiah 6:1-14.

18. Discuss the two traps attempted against Nehemiah and his response to each.

- Vv. 1-9—

- Vv. 10-14—

Historical Insight: Another proof of Sanballat's dishonest intentions is that he sent *an open letter*, i.e., not sealed, as was the custom in those days. With the open letter, which could be read by anyone on the way, he was responsible for the further spreading of the rumor. (Dr. Constable's Notes on Nehemiah 2019 Edition, p.36)

Read Nehemiah 6:15-19.

19. What do you learn from these verses?

So the wall was completed on the twenty-fifth of Elul, in fifty-two days. When all our enemies heard about this, all the surrounding nations were afraid and lost their self-confidence, because they realized that this work had been done with the help of our God. (Nehemiah 6:15-16)

20. ***Your life's journey:*** Nehemiah was a special man for a special time, but that also can be said for each of us. Where do you think God has placed you to be a servant leader in order to accomplish His purposes? Or, what position and/or responsibility do you hold that might be useful in bringing about good in the lives you touch?

Respond to the Lord about what He's shown you today.

Recommended: *Listen to the podcast "The Two Aspects of Trusting God" after doing this lesson to reinforce what you have learned. Use the listener guide on the next page.*

The Two Aspects of Trusting God

Has God placed something in your heart for you to do for Him?

Whatever it is involves two aspects of trusting God. The first one is that you must trust him as you step forward and do your part His way. And, the second aspect is that you must trust him to do His part in the areas over which you have no control. Those two aspects of trusting God are necessary to act on whatever God has placed in your heart to do. The book of Nehemiah provides a beautiful illustration of this for us.

THE SEED WAS PLANTED BY GOD IN NEHEMIAH'S HEART

- Nehemiah's distress from the news of Jerusalem's disgrace led him to pray about what to do. God placed into Nehemiah's heart the desire to go and repair the walls and gates of Jerusalem.

- Just before he approached the king of Persia about this, Nehemiah asked for God to be with him as he did his part (speaking to the king), and he asked for God to do God's part in directing the heart and mind of the king. Those are the two aspects of trusting God.

- When God places something in your heart to do, especially when it involves someone else and situations over which you have no control, you must trust God to lead you in what you choose to do. You want to do your part His way, not your own way or the world's way.

THE TIME HAD COME TO ACT

After the seed was planted, the time had come to act. When Nehemiah was asked by the king what he wanted to do, Nehemiah sent up a quick prayer before he answered (Nehemiah 2:4). God took care of His part by directing the king's heart and mind to be favorable to Nehemiah's requests. Nehemiah asked for letters to all the authorities for safe travel and materials needed to do the job. That was Nehemiah's part to make the official requests. God worked through the authorities to grant Nehemiah's requests and give him authority to do the work in Jerusalem (Nehemiah 2:7-9). Once again, the narrative demonstrates the two aspects of trusting God. Yet, opposition tested Nehemiah's trust.

OPPOSITION TESTED NEHEMIAH'S TRUST

Though Nehemiah was completely trusting God and doing things God's way, God didn't stop the opposition. Nehemiah knew without a doubt that God had given him the vision to rebuild and that God's gracious hand was upon him with every step. Yet, God didn't make it easy for Nehemiah and the Israelites to do what He called them to do.

- The opposition tried **intimidation**. Nehemiah led the people in prayer for God to do His part in giving them protection. But, they also did their part by posting guards day and night and carrying weapons with them while they worked.

- The opposition tried **fake news**. Nehemiah called the news a lie and probably informed his boss, the king, that it was fake news.

- The opposition tried **deception**. Nehemiah didn't fall for either one of the traps, including the fake news spoken by a woman who claimed to be a prophet. Beware whose side you are on when you give information.

- The opposition then tried to hit Nehemiah by fostering **disloyalty** from within. The Jewish nobility had even refused to do the work on the walls, disdaining such manual labor. Nehemiah prayed and later confronted them with their hypocrisy and their disloyalty to God and His people.

- God gave Nehemiah what he needed to respond to the opposition. Nehemiah needed discernment for each of these weapons to recognize the error and to avoid an improper response. Nehemiah needed God's strength to combat the weapons. He prayed, "Lord, strengthen my hands" (Nehemiah 6:9). Nehemiah trusted in God while at the same time taking safety precautions. There is nothing wrong with acting wisely for prevention and protection from danger while trusting God for that protection.

- God doesn't stop the opposition so that we will learn to rely on Him more than on ourselves. Relying on Him, even when waiting for the right moment to act, is still trusting Him while we are doing our part (which is waiting and praying), knowing that He is working on His part (which is whatever that situation requires). *2 Corinthians 1:9*

THE TWO ASPECTS OF TRUSTING GOD

What has God placed on your heart to do for others?

- Is it raising children to know and love Him and choose to follow Him as adults? Trust Him to lead you to follow godly child-rearing principles and actions while you trust Him to work in the hearts of your children.

- Is it managing people or a project at work (Nehemiah's experience was a workplace task with the king as the CEO.) Trust God to lead you to act with honesty and integrity among your fellow employees and managers while you trust Him to work in their hearts as well.

- Is it serving in a local ministry with teens or special needs or homeless people? Whatever it is, trust God to lead you to speak and act with compassion while you trust Him to work to meet the needs of those you are serving.

Trust God while you do your part His way and trust Him to do His part alongside what you are doing. Those are the two aspects of trusting God.

We can have hope because we have God with us. So, remember our lane markers for the race.

- #1. Choose to persevere through every challenge.
- #2. Count on God's promise to give you hope.
- #3. Let that hope sustain you through the rough-and-tumble of life.
- #4. Celebrate the joyful reward.

Let Jesus satisfy your heart with hope so you can persevere through life.

11 Building More Than A Wall

Nehemiah 7-13

For everything that was written in the past was written to teach us, so that through the endurance taught in the Scriptures and the encouragement they provide we might have hope. (Romans 15:4, NIV)

DAY ONE STUDY

Read Nehemiah 6:15-16 and 7:1-5. Ask the Lord Jesus to teach you through His Word.

1. What choices and actions do you observe Nehemiah taking now that the wall is built?

The rest of chapter 7 lists the families who had returned to Judah from the exile in Babylon. The first 9 chapters of 1 Chronicles contains the descendants and settlement locations for each of the 12 tribes of Israel. This helped people to know where to settle back on their families' lands. The exile lasted 70 years, so many of them had never lived there before this time.

Especially listed in Nehemiah chapter 7 are the priests, Levites, gatekeepers, and temple servants who returned from the exile. The restored nation needed priests who could prove their ancestry so they could serve at the rebuilt temple. No hearsay allowed (Nehemiah 7:63-65). Only those who descended from Aaron, Moses' brother, could be priests at the Temple.

The group called "the Levites" were those from the tribe of Levi who did not descend from Aaron. They had other duties to perform and were collectively called "the Levites" to distinguish them from the priests. The Levites were like local pastors for communities as well as servants for all aspects of the Tabernacle and Temple including security (gatekeepers) and leading worship. They were supported by their own farms as well as by tithes given to the Lord. In order to reestablish worship of God in the land, those who returned from exile had to prove their lineage in order to serve in either capacity.

> **Focus on the Meaning:** Nehemiah not only led the people of Judah to rebuild the walls of their city; he had led them to renewed commitment to God and to His revealed will...Rebuilding the walls of Jerusalem had given the people a new sense of their identity as God's people. Success despite opposition had helped them realize that their God was truly among them, as small as their people and land had become. (*The Teacher's Commentary*, pp. 308, 310)

Read Nehemiah 8:1-12.

> **Historical Insight:** This assembly took place just six days after the completion of the walls (October 8, 445 BC). The seventh month is the beginning of the Jewish civil year and was marked by a celebration known as the Feast of Trumpets (described in Numbers 29). Ezra was a priest and a scribe, one who "had devoted himself to the study and observance of the Law of the Lord (Ezra 7:10)." Ezra had led a group of exiles from Babylon to Judah 13 years before Nehemiah's arrival. The books of Ezra and Nehemiah are actually one book in the Hebrew Bible and contain eyewitness accounts written by the two principal characters.

As an effective leader, Nehemiah knew when to delegate responsibility of leading to other qualified people. Nehemiah was the governor of Judah and knew how to lead the people publicly. But, the walls were not an end. Rebuilding Israel also required a solid foundation for their spiritual health. Ezra was the priest, the one designated by God to lead the people spiritually.

2. Describe the scene from vv. 1-5.

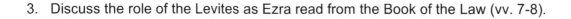

3. Discuss the role of the Levites as Ezra read from the Book of the Law (vv. 7-8).

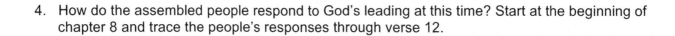

4. How do the assembled people respond to God's leading at this time? Start at the beginning of chapter 8 and trace the people's responses through verse 12.

> **Scriptural Insight:** The people asked Ezra the priest to bring the book of the Law of the Lord and to read it to them. This would undoubtedly be the entire Pentateuch—the first five books of the Bible: Genesis, Exodus, Leviticus, Numbers and Deuteronomy. This indicates the tremendous desire of these people for the truth. They listened, while standing, from daybreak until noon! Certainly, this long attention indicates how deeply they were aware of their ignorance about life and how much they needed answers from God. (Ray Stedman, Sermon Notes, January 1989)

5. The people responded to the word of the Lord with deep emotion and weeping. Then, Nehemiah told the people in v. 10, "This day is holy to our Lord. Do not grieve, for the joy of the Lord is your strength." Biblical joy is an inner gladness despite outward circumstances. What do you think Nehemiah meant by what he said in v. 10?

6. ***Your life's journey:*** Recall the problems and challenges of Nehemiah 1-6 covered in the last lesson. God's people went through tough times, yet there was a time for celebration and joy. What do you celebrate? What brings you joy?

Respond to the Lord about what He's shown you today.

DAY TWO STUDY

Read Nehemiah chapter 9. Ask the Lord Jesus to teach you through His Word.

The Israelites assembled again 24 days later for a time of confession of sin and renewal of their commitment to worship Yahweh only. The prayer in chapter 9 is the longest recorded prayer in the Bible and is similar to Psalms 78, 105-106 in how it recalls the highlights of Israel's history. Some of us are inclined to be indifferent to history, but as you read this prayer, observe the very personal involvement of God in the history of the Jewish people and remember that God does not change. God is the same yesterday, today and forever.

7. Who was present that day (9:1-2; 10:28)?

Scriptural Insight: Women and children attended important occasions like this, especially when the Word of God was being publicly read. You can see this throughout Kings and Chronicles. Renewal of their faith as a people involved the whole family.

8. What do you learn about God's power and His goodness from this prayer?

- In creation (v. 6)—

- To Abraham (vv. 7-8)—

- During the Exodus (vv. 9-21)—

- In the promised land (vv. 22-28)—

- Through the prophets (vv. 29-31)—

- In their present situation (vv. 23-29)—

9. ***Deeper Discoveries (optional):*** Write our own prayer recalling God's faithfulness through the years to you.

Read Nehemiah 9:38; 10:28-39.

In essence, the prayer you just read is a rededication of the nation to serve their God. The people choose to renew the covenant between themselves as a people and God. The beginning of chapter 10 lists all the leaders of the people who put their names to the agreement. Nehemiah, as governor, was the first one to affix his seal of approval and commitment to the agreement.

10. What did the men, women, and children agree to do in this rededication?

Think About It: In both Old and New Testament times, God seeks people who want to enjoy an honest relationship with Him. "For the eyes of the Lord range throughout the earth to strengthen those whose hearts are fully committed to him (2 Chronicles 16:9)."

11. *Your life's journey:* Someone once said, "Efficiency is doing things right. Effectiveness is doing the *right things.*" Nehemiah, as a leader led a great many people to do the right thing in their relationship to God, in their relationships with each other, and in their responsibilities to their communities. God has given each of us people whose lives are intertwined with ours as well. Some of those people (younger, older, or the same age) follow us. Think about the ones who are following you.

- How do you normally react to sin in their lives?

- What do you do to lead them to do the right thing ...

  In their relationship to God?

  In their relationships with other Christians?

  As responsible members of their community?

Respond to the Lord about what He's shown you today.

DAY THREE STUDY

The city of Jerusalem grew. Chapters 11 and 12 of Nehemiah detail this growth. By the way, Zerubbabel, son of Shealtiel (12:1), was in the line of David. So, when he returned to Israel after the exile (93 years before the time of Nehemiah), Zerubbabel represented the kingship of Israel even though the Persian government did not let Israel have its own king. Jeshua was the High Priest who returned with Zerubbabel leading thousands of people with them.

> *Now the leaders of the people lived in Jerusalem, but the rest of the people cast lots to bring one out of ten to live in Jerusalem, the holy city, while nine-tenths remained in other cities. And the people blessed the men who volunteered to remain in Jerusalem. (Nehemiah 11:1,2)*

The wall has been built, the gates are hung, the city is now well-defended and filled with people. The time for dedication and celebration has come.

Read Nehemiah 12:27-43. Ask the Lord Jesus to teach you through His Word.

12. In Nehemiah 4:3, Tobiah mocked the working Israelites by saying that "if even a fox climbed on it, he would break down their wall of stones." Nehemiah proved him wrong! Describe the celebration in your own words,

> **Think About It:** Until Christ returns, this world will be a place of trouble and difficulty. Yet, it is right at times to stop, give thanks, and celebrate what God has done.

After the celebration, Nehemiah reestablished the temple service as David had organized it, appointing men from the Levites for all the various duties. And, the Israelites brought in their tithes and offerings for the support of the priests and Levites. The Book of Moses was read aloud to all the people. Unbelieving foreigners, especially Ammonites and Moabites, were excluded from the assembly of Israel. After 12 years of serving in Jerusalem, Nehemiah went back to Persian for a short time. Upon his return, he discovered that the Israelites had gone back again to some wicked behaviors. It is thought that the prophet Malachi spoke to the people during this time.

Read Nehemiah 13:4-31.

We'll look at some of the ways the people fell back into disobedience and how Nehemiah responded. Notice how Nehemiah's enemies Tobiah and Sanballat kept popping up like thorns!

13. Focus on vv. 4-9:

- What wickedness happened?

- What is Nehemiah's response?

14. Focus on vv. 10-14 (also 10:32, 39):

  - What wickedness happened?

  - What is Nehemiah's response?

15. Focus on vv. 15-22 (also 10:3):

  - What wickedness happened?

  - What is Nehemiah's response?

16. Focus on vv. 23-31 (also 10:30):

  - What wickedness happened?

  - What is Nehemiah's response?

Think About It: Nehemiah's actions were extreme. Chuck Swindoll offers the following comments on what he calls "taking problems by the throat." Nehemiah faced the wrong head-on. He dealt with the wrong severely. Nehemiah worked toward a permanent correction and always followed up with prayer…The final scene in Nehemiah's book portrays him on his knees asking God for grace. He fought hard for the right, but he had kept his heart soft before the Lord. What a magnificent model of leadership. He was a man of honesty, conviction and devotion. (Chuck Swindoll, *Hand Me Another Brick*, p. 179)

17. *Your life's journey:* What in Nehemiah's life encourages you to persevere?

FINISHING WELL

Read Hebrews 12:1-3.

18. This has been our key passage for the study. What does it mean to you now to run the race of life with PERSEVERANCE?

May God continually bless you as you run with PERSEVERANCE the race set before you.

Think About It: You can't grow in grace in a classroom, through a seminar, or during a "quiet time," as good as those things may be...You can only grow in grace through a personal relationship with the Lord Jesus Christ, who teaches you truth from His Word, which you then take out into the rough-and-tumble of real life in the real world. The "curriculum" cannot be planned or anticipated...Whatever the situations in your life may be, that is where you will have to grow in grace...in spite of our personal failures and sins... as we focus on what God is doing in the midst of what we are doing. (Bob George, *Growing in Grace,* pp. 13-15*)*

Respond to the Lord about what He's shown you today.

Recommended: *Listen to the podcast "The Joy of the Lord Is Your Strength" after doing this lesson to reinforce what you have learned. Use the listener guide on the next page.*

The Joy of the Lord Is Your Strength

For the joy set before him, our Lord Jesus Christ endured the shame and pain of the cross. And, in that time of extreme trouble, Jesus looked ahead to the joy He would experience after He persevered through His earthly life. Joy is a reward for perseverance.

WHAT IS JOY?

- Most people define joy as a feeling of happiness when you're smiling and laughing a lot. And, they think that happiness comes from "good happenings." But, what happens if things are not so good? Can you really have joy then?

- The word "joy in the Bible refers to having a **deep inner gladness, regardless of the circumstances** going on around you. That means whether you are rich or poor, sick or healthy, successful or struggling, you can still have a feeling of gladness or pleasure deep down inside. Now, you may not feel like smiling on the outside, but you can still smile on the inside.

JOY IS IN GOD'S CHARACTER.

- God has joy whenever anyone comes to Him to have his or her sins forgiven by faith in His Son Jesus. The Bible describes lots of rejoicing in heaven at that time.

- God has pleasure in His creation. We see that in Job and In Psalms a lot. The Father God has joy in what His hands have made, especially His creatures. That includes you. Does that make you smile inside to think that God finds pleasure in you?

- God expresses His joy. In His love for you, God rejoices over you with singing. He takes delight in you because you trust in Him. *Zephaniah 3:17*

GOD GIVES US HIS JOY.

- A sense of joy pervades the Bible. It is seen as the enthusiastic response of the community worshiping and praising God. It's seen as people celebrate who God is and what He has done for them in the past.

- God's joy comes to us from a relationship with Him through knowing Jesus Christ. Jesus, who was God, had God's joy **in** Him. Jesus promised to give His joy to His disciples so that it would be in them, also. *John 15:11*

- God's joy is given to those who have not seen Jesus but have believed in Him. The moment you believe in Jesus Christ, the Holy Spirit comes to live inside of you. And, He gives you God's glorious, uncontainable joy as a fruit of His presence. *1 Peter 1:8*

GOD'S JOY MAKES US STRONG.

The joy of the Lord is God's joy. He has it, and when He gives it to His people, it makes them strong.

- God's joy makes us strong in giving us the assurance of His presence during the best times of life and during those miserable, painful times of life.

- God's joy in us gives us the courage to face tough times because we know He is with us. Jesus is our example of how to endure difficulties, so we won't grow weary and lose heart.

- God's joy in us gives us hope and confidence in what God is doing in any situation. So, we can have the ability to smile on the inside even if things are going wrong on the outside.

- God's joy wells up within us and motivates us to serve others in love. We want to share His joy so that others will experience His joy, too.

GOD'S JOY LEADS US TO SHARE IN GOD'S DELIGHT

- God's joy leads us to take pleasure or delight in the same things that delight God. We delight in justice. We delight in approaching life God's way more than our own way or the world's way. We delight in studying His Word the Bible, in doing what pleases Him, and in praising Him.

- It is not wrong for a Christian to have pleasure or to seek pleasure. It is only wrong to seek pleasure in the things that are selfish. Christians filled with God's joy should find many reasons to laugh and delight in life. We can serve God with delight. We can love our families and friends with delight. We can enjoy nature.

- We can celebrate God's goodness to us. Celebration is a biblical concept. God often called His people together for a time of celebration. It was woven into the fabric of their calendars so they would remember God's goodness to them. Why not have a yearly celebration of the time when we trusted in Christ or chose to commit our lives to him?

- One day, our joy will be even greater in heaven when we are with Jesus and can have the delight of seeing Him with our own eyes. Oh, glorious joy!

We can have hope because we have God with us. So, remember our lane markers for the race.

#1. Choose to persevere through every challenge.
#2. Count on God's promise to give you hope.
#3. Let that hope sustain you through the rough-and-tumble of life.
#4. Celebrate the joyful reward.

Let Jesus satisfy your heart with hope so you can persevere through life.

> Keep reading to get a peek at Lesson One of the next study in "Fear to Faith Walk" series, Perspective: Insights from 1 and 2 Thessalonians. Having the biblical perspective on your work and your future will help you to continue walking from fear to faith.

Preview of "Perspective: Insights from 1 and 2 Thessalonians"

Lesson 1: Overview of 1 and 2 Thessalonians

LISTEN TO THE PODCAST: **THE NEED FOR PERSPECTIVE**

> **Recommended:** *Listen to the podcast "The Need for Perspective" as an introduction to the whole study. Use the following listener guide.*

The story

When the apostle Paul wrote the letters that we know as 1 and 2 Thessalonians, he had been a Christian for more than 15 years. From the beginning, Jesus told Paul that he was to go to those who were called Gentiles (non-Jews) and preach the gospel to them.

On his second missionary journey, God directed their movements first to northern Greece to the cities of Philippi and Thessalonica. Then, they went to southern Greece to the cities of Athens and Corinth. It is from Corinth that Paul wrote two letters back to the Thessalonians.

Gain perspective

> Perspective is an objective assessment of any situation, giving all aspects their comparative importance.

We all need perspective to help us successfully navigate through the challenges of daily life. Gaining perspective is like sharpening your focus with a lens. Sharpening your focus not only clears up blurry vision, but it can also help you to see something at a distance that you were not able to see. You get a glimpse of where you are heading. Paul's letters to the Thessalonian Christians helped them gain perspective about many issues of life.

From the moment Paul entered their city, the Thessalonians knew him as being well-educated and a tent-making craftsman. They knew that he was determined, bold, convinced of the truth of Christ, and very committed to Jesus' calling on his life. He was a gifted teacher and loved God's people almost as much as he loved God Himself. Paul reminded them of that in 1 Thessalonians to help sharpen their focus on who he was and what kind of relationship he had with them. They could trust his words.

There were no cell phones or email for Paul. He depended upon letters and eyewitness accounts for his information about all the churches. You'll see evidence of this in the Thessalonian letters. Biblical perspective on life is God's perspective on life. Paul helped the Thessalonians gain God's perspective on the persecution they were suffering at the hands of their neighbors. When you sharpen your focus to gain perspective, you get...

> ...the ability to see God's presence, to perceive God's power, and to focus on God's plan in spite of the obstacles. (Chuck Swindoll, *Insight for Today devotional*, May 19, 2017)

Biblical perspective on life helps you grow in confidence because you learn that your self-worth is not derived from any human being but from God.

Biblical perspective about death and the future gives you hope and assurance of your future with Christ in eternity. You will not fear death as those who have no hope.

Knowing the future hope gives you God's perspective on life that you need in your world today. For now, you must live and work in this world. Paul's letters to the Thessalonians have a lot to say about that.

When you gain the biblical perspective on who God is, what it means to live your life to please Him, and what He has planned for your future, you get a security in Him that allows you to rest and enjoy life today. And, you will be able to serve God with greater enthusiasm and freedom to impact your world for Him.

Let Jesus satisfy your heart with His perspective on life in the present and in the future. Then, live securely in Him during this time of waiting.

DAY ONE STUDY

Ask the Lord Jesus to teach you through His Word.

The ABCs of 1 and 2 Thessalonians—Author, Background, and Context

Like any book you read, it always helps to know a bit about the author, the background setting for the story (i.e., past, present, future), and where the book fits into a series (that's the context). The same is true of Bible books.

AUTHOR

Paul identifies himself as the author of this letter written to the church of the Thessalonians. Paul, whose Hebrew name was Saul, was born in Tarsus, a major Roman city on the coast of southeast Asia Minor. Tarsus was the center for the tent-making industry. Paul was trained in that craft as his occupation (his primary paying profession). As a Jewish Pharisee from the tribe of Benjamin, Paul was educated at the feet of Gamaliel, a well-respected rabbi of the day. Paul was an ardent persecutor of the early church until his life-changing encounter with Jesus Christ.

After believing in Jesus Christ as his Savior, Paul was called by Christ to take the gospel to the Gentiles. This was an amazing about-face for a committed Pharisee like Paul who ordinarily would have nothing to do with Gentiles. He founded numerous churches and wrote 13 letters that are included in the New Testament. Tradition has it that Paul was beheaded shortly after he wrote 2 Timothy in 67 AD. *(Adapted from Acts 8:3; 9:1-31; 22:3-5; 26:9-11; and Galatians 1:11-24.)*

BACKGROUND

Located in northern Greece, Thessalonica was founded in 315 BC. Over time, it became an important urban center because of its strategic location near the Aegean Sea. In the Roman Empire, it was the capital of the province of Macedonia and its largest city with 200,000 people. Thessalonica stood on the *Via Egnatia*, the Roman version of an interstate highway, making it an important city of commerce. In Paul's day, it was a self-governing community with enough Jews in residence to warrant a synagogue (Acts 17:1).

While Paul was in Troas on his second missionary journey, God showed him a vision of a man from Macedonia saying, "Come over and help us." Paul and Silas went, stopping first at Philippi, where they preached the gospel, and a church was formed. After spending a night in prison for driving an evil spirit from a girl, Paul and Silas were forced to leave Philippi. They went about 100 miles west to Thessalonica.

For at least three Sabbath days, Paul reasoned in the synagogue with those present, and many believed the gospel. Because of all that he accomplished in Thessalonica, he probably ministered for a longer time than just three weeks. Several Jews and many God-fearing Greeks believed, including some leading women of the city. This angered a group of unbelieving Jews who then stirred up trouble for Paul. So, the Thessalonian Christians sent Paul, Silas, and Timothy away from the city by night to Berea, 50 miles to the west.

Paul and his party began their evangelistic work in Berea in the synagogue, as was their custom, and many people there believed. Sadly, the Thessalonian Jews traveled to Berea and stirred up more trouble for Paul. So, the Berean Christians sent Paul away to Athens (southern Greece). But, Silas and Timothy remained in Berea. While in Athens, Paul wrote to Silas and Timothy, asking them to join him there. But, he soon sent Silas back to Philippi and Timothy back to Thessalonica to continue discipling those churches. Then, Paul moved to Corinth. Silas and Timothy rejoined him there, bringing a financial gift from the Christians in those Macedonian (northern Greece) towns. Timothy's report of conditions in the Thessalonian church led Paul to write the first letter from Corinth about 51 AD. Then, he wrote the second letter within 6-12 months after the first letter.

Here is a possible timeline (a best guess based on available information):

- Church founded: Fall/Winter 50-51 (Acts 17:1-15)
- Paul sent Timothy to Thessalonica: Spring 51 (1 Thessalonians 3:2)
- Paul in Corinth: Summer 51 (Acts 18:1-5)
- Timothy came with news from Thessalonica
- 1 Thessalonians written and sent: Fall 51
- News received
- 2 Thessalonians written and sent: Winter/Spring 52

CONTEXT

Even though you will find 1 and 2 Thessalonians after the book of Colossians in the New Testament, the Thessalonian letters were written much earlier. In fact, they are considered to be some of the earliest of Paul's writings. Only Galatians was likely written before them. Because of the short time between the writing of the 2 letters to the Thessalonians, it makes sense to study them together as we'll be doing.

1. What grabbed your attention as you read the ABC's of the books of 1 and 2 Thessalonians?

2. Read Acts 17:1-15. What do you learn from these verses about Paul's experience in Thessalonica?

- Vv. 1-5—

- Vv. 6-10, 13—

- What events and people would still be fresh in his mind just a few months later when he wrote the letters?

Scriptural Insight: Paul's reasoning "persuaded some" in the synagogue services. His converts seem to have been mainly Gentiles, many of whom were God-fearers, or "God-fearing Greeks," but some of them were Jews. "Jason" (v. 5), Aristarchus, and Secundus appear to have been among these new believers. The "leading women" could have belonged to the upper classes, or they may have been the wives of the city's leading men. In either case, the gospel had an impact on the leadership level of society in Thessalonica. ... Three converts from Thessalonica—Sopater, Aristarchus (Acts 20:4; 27:2; Col. 4:10), and Secundus (Acts 20:4)—later traveled with Paul (Acts 20:4). Aristarchus stayed with Paul during his Caesarean imprisonment and traveled with him all the way to Rome. (*Dr. Constable's Notes on Acts 2020 Edition,* adapted from pp. 347, 350, 481)

Gain Perspective

You've probably heard the phrase, "You need to gain perspective." But, what is perspective? According to the dictionary:

Perspective is an objective assessment of any situation, giving all aspects their comparative importance.

Objective assessment. Looking at all the issues and facts. That sounds like a necessary action to take whenever you must make a decision, doesn't it? We all need perspective to help us successfully navigate through the challenges of daily life.

Gaining perspective is like sharpening your focus with a lens. When you have trouble seeing, and you go to an optometrist to get your eyes checked, you come away with a prescription for glasses or contacts that will enable your eyes to focus again. When you put on those new lenses, what was once a blur has now become clear. That's what happens when you gain perspective.

Sharpening your focus not only clears up blurry vision, but it can also help us to see something at a distance that we were not able to see. Consider how a pair of binoculars works. Let's say you are driving down a highway to get to the mountains. You go around a curve, and there they are in the distance. You get excited about your journey there. But, you need help to see them. So, you pull out a pair of binoculars and focus on the mountain peaks in the distance. You get a glimpse of where you are heading.

That's what Paul's letters to the Thessalonian Christians helped them to do. They gained perspective about a bunch of things.

Biblical perspective on life is God's perspective on life. Paul helped the Thessalonians gain God's perspective on the persecution they were suffering at the hands of their neighbors. Having the biblical perspective about suffering helps you to stand firm and press onward regardless of obstacles in your life.

Biblical perspective on life helps you grow in confidence because you learn that your self-worth is not derived from any human being but from God. This gives you stability, certainty, and confidence in your God who is faithful to you. Others will notice and be benefited by this.

The Thessalonians had questions about death and the future. Biblical perspective about that gives you hope and assurance of your future with Christ in eternity. You will not fear death as those who have no hope. And, if you like eschatology (prophecy about the end times, especially Jesus' return), you'll enjoy Paul's letters to the Thessalonians. As you study Paul's letters to the Thessalonians, you will gain some perspective on the future that God has planned for all believers as well as for human history. One-fourth of 1 Thessalonians and nearly half of 2 Thessalonians deal with the coming of Christ from heaven for His own and the Great Tribulation on earth that will occur afterwards. You will gain perspective on the end times and how to view evil in the present. We will enjoy our time of discovery when we get to those passages.

Knowing the future hope gives you God's perspective on life that you need in your world today. For now, you must live and work in this world. Paul's letters to the Thessalonians have a lot to say about your daily life, including your work. You can view work as worship and see purpose in it when you gain God's perspective.

When you gain the biblical perspective on who God is, what it means to live your life to please Him, and what He has planned for your future, you get a security in Him that allows you to rest and enjoy life today. Who wouldn't want that kind of security? And, you will be able to serve God with greater enthusiasm and freedom to impact your world for Him.

3. In what areas of your life do you need perspective right now?

Respond to the Lord about what you learned today.

DAY TWO STUDY—GET THE BIG PICTURE OF 1 THESSALONIANS

Ask the Lord Jesus to teach you through His Word.

In all of our *Joyful Walk Bible Studies*, we follow the inductive process for Bible Study. The inductive process starts with observation, looking carefully at what the text actually says. ***What does the Bible say?*** The next step is interpretation, which is trying to understand the author's intended meaning—to him and to the audience who would read or hear it. ***What does it mean?*** Once you know what the Bible says and what it means, then you are ready for application, which is learning how to live this out in your life. ***What application will you make?*** When you follow the inductive process for Bible Study, you will be able to confidently dwell in that truth.

What does the Bible say? *(This is the "Observation" step in the process of Bible Study.)*

Where do we begin? Have you ever heard the saying, "You can't see the forest for the trees?"

The best way to study any book of the Bible is to begin with the "forest" (survey the whole) and then proceed to the "trees" (the individual parts). We will start by getting an overview of what Paul wrote in his letters to the Thessalonians. Since they were written so close together in time, we will read them both this week to get the continuity of thought. We will read them as they were intended—a letter from one dear friend to another.

Today, read the letter called 1 Thessalonians at one sitting. It will take about 10 minutes. You can read the letter in any translation of the Bible you choose. A copy of each letter (NIV translation) is included in this study guide before Lesson One. Feel free to mark anything that grabs your attention, and look for the main topics. Then, answer the questions below.

4. What one thing do you remember most from your reading of this letter?

5. What would you say were the main subjects that Paul covered in this letter?

6. What issues seem to be bothering the Thessalonian church?

7. What questions do you have after reading 1 Thessalonians that you would like to have answered in this study?

Respond to the Lord about what you learned today.

Get *Perspective* at melanienewton.com as well
as most online bookstores.

Sources

1. Douglas, J.D. and Merrill C. Tenney. *The NIV Compact Dictionary of the Bible*

2. Durant, Jayme. *Acts & Facts,* 48 (11)

3. Edmund, Raymond Edmund. *In Quietness and Confidence*

4. George, Bob. *Growing in Grace*

5. Lewis, C. S. *Reflections on the Psalms*

6. *Life Application Study Bible*

7. Murphy, Kris. *God Reveals We Respond*

8. Ryrie, Charles. *Ryrie Study Bible*, 1995 expanded edition

9. Stedman, Ray. *Sermon Notes*, January 1989

10. Tenney, Merrill. *The Zondervan Pictorial Bible Dictionary*

11. *The Teacher's Commentary*

12. Swindoll, Charles. *David*

13. Swindoll, Charles. David, Bible study guide

14. Swindoll, Charles. *Elijah, Bible study guide*

15. Swindoll, Charles. *Hand Me Another Brick*

16. Vine, W.E., Merrill F. Unger, and William White, Jr. *Vines Complete Expository Dictionary of Old and New Testament Words*

17. Walvoord, John and Roy Zuck. *Bible Knowledge Commentary Old Testament*

18. Wilkinson, Bruce. *Talk through the Bible*

Quotations from Oswald Chambers, Chuck Swindoll, and Jonathan Edwards are named but not sourced.

Made in the USA
Monee, IL
08 June 2021